Sing a New Creation

A Supplement to Common Praise (1998)

Anglican Church of Canada

CHURCH
PUBLISHING
INCORPORATED

General Synod of the Anglican Church of Canada
80 Hayden Street, Toronto, Ontario, Canada, M4Y 3G2
publications@national.anglican.ca

Church Publishing
19 East 34th Street
New York, NY 10016

A record of this book is available from the Library of Congress.

ISBN-13: 978-1-64065-273-6 (paperback)

Table of Contents

Introduction

Sing A New Creation has been designed to supplement *Common Praise*, the current hymn book of the Anglican Church of Canada. The selection of its contents was guided by several aims: to respond to the particular needs communicated to us by congregations from across the country; to include songs and settings that are attractive and enjoyable to sing; to include texts and tunes by Canadian Anglican writers and composers; and to reflect the global character of the church by including a wide range of material from diverse cultures and language groups.

While denominational hymn books like *Common Praise* aim to be comprehensive, including all of the hymns and service music needed by the church for a generation or more, the purpose of a hymn book supplement like *Sing A New Creation* is to expand, refresh and enliven the church's existing singing practice, responding to changing needs and reflecting recent musical developments. Thus the compilers of a hymn book supplement enjoy a degree of freedom in selecting material for inclusion that committees creating a more comprehensive collections do not.

We hope that congregations will exercise a similar freedom in how they make use of the collection. Worship planners will find *Sing A New Creation* to be a rich resource for selecting hymns for their traditional roles in Anglican liturgy such as Processional, Offertory, Communion and Recessional. But the collection should also be perused with an openness that allows the pieces themselves to suggest possible ways they can be used. Some of the possibilities: singing at congregational meetings and social events; teaching songs by rote to children; singing before the beginning of the liturgy either in place of or in addition to the instrumental prelude; crafting brief litanies with sung response that speak to current congregational concerns; using individual verses or refrains as prayer responses.

While many of the hymns and songs in *Sing A New Creation* can be accompanied by organ, others should not be. Some songs are included here with only melody line and chord symbols to be sung with guitar. Others will be found to be more suitable to accompaniment by piano than by organ. Songs from the global church can be enriched and more authentically sung by including percussion or melody instruments and omitting chordal accompaniment altogether.

A significant recent development in congregational song is the practice of so-called "paperless" singing, in which songs are taught and led without the need for singers to read either text or music from the printed page. The benefits of this practice quickly become obvious: the possibility of more direct engagement in the music, greater bodily freedom, and a greater sense congregational singing as a genuinely communal action. Not every hymn or song is appropriate for this approach. Singing "by ear" in this way work best with songs that are shorter, have a minimum of text to remember, and include repetitive musical patterns. Hymns and songs especially appropriate for singing by ear are indicated by the symbol ⓟ found near the bottom right-hand corner of the page.

The organization of *Sing A New Creation* follows that of *Common Praise* with a few notable differences. Hymns suitable for Gathering open the collection, and Sending hymns can be found near the end of the congregational song section of the book. In addition, the subject heading Praise has been changed to Praise and Lament, where hymns of both types are interspersed. In recent years the church has become aware that the tradition of lament has been neglected and needs to be recovered as part of its language of worship. Lament is not a negation or the opposite of praise. Indeed, biblical lament almost always concludes with an expression of confidence in and praise of God. But it also gives expression to the experiences of suffering and darkness that are an integral part of human life. Paul Gibson has said that "lament is the shadow side of praise". It is entirely appropriate that the singing of a lament be one of the options considered by liturgical planners for the act of praise during The Gathering of the Community in the BAS Eucharist.

Considerations of space have limited the number and format of the indexes found at the back of the book. It is anticipated that additional and expanded indexes, as well as notes on performance will appear in due course on the web sites of both the Anglican Church of Canada and of Church Publishing, Inc.

– Kenneth Hull, convener

Hymn Book Supplement Task Force
Kenneth Hull, convener
David Buley
*John Campbell
Michael Capon
*Douglas Cowling
*Deirdre Piper
Martha Tatarnic
Becca Whitla
    *served during part of the project

Reviewers
David Harrison
Gordon Johnston

Consultant
Mark MacDonald

Staff
Eileen Scully

Typesetting and Copyright Permissions
Selah Publishing Co., Inc.
    David Schaap, president
    Virginia Schaap, vice-president

O Breath of Life

1 O Breath of Life, come sweep - ing through us, re - vive your church with life and
2 O Wind of God, come bend us, break us, till hum - bly we con - fess our
3 O Song of Love, come sing with - in us, re - new - ing thought and will and

pow'r; O Breath of Life, come, cleanse, re -
need; then in your ten - der strength re -
heart; come, Love of Christ, a - fresh to

new us, and fit your church to meet this hour.
make us, re - vive, re - store— for this we plead.
win us, re - vive your church in ev - ery part!

*For a four-part texture, tenors can double the melody an octave lower
and altos can double the bass line an octave higher.*

Text: Elizabeth Ann Porter Head, 1920, alt.
Music: James E. Clemens, 2001, ©.

98 98
SPIRIT WIND

2 Longing for Light

Unison

1 Long-ing for light, we wait in dark-ness. Long-ing for
2 Long-ing for peace, our world is troub-led. Long-ing for
3 Long-ing for food, man-y are hun-gry. Long-ing for
4 Long-ing for shel-ter, man-y are home-less. Long-ing for
5 Man-y the gifts, man-y the peo-ple, man-y the

truth, we turn to you. Make us your own,
hope, man-y de-spair. Your word a-lone
wa-ter, man-y still thirst. Make us your bread,
warmth, man-y are cold. Make us your build-ing,
hearts that yearn to be-long. Let us be ser-vants

your ho-ly peo-ple, light for the world to see.
has power to save us. Make us your liv-ing voice.
bro-ken for oth-ers, shared un-til all are fed.
shel-ter-ing oth-ers, walls made of liv-ing stone.
to one an-oth-er, mak-ing your king-dom come.

Text and music: Bernadette Farrell, 1993, ©, *admin. OCP Publications.*

98 96 with refrain
CHRIST BE OUR LIGHT

Refrain

Christ, be our light! Shine in our hearts.

Shine through the dark - ness. Christ, be our light!

Shine in your Church gather-ed to - day.

last time

3 Come and Find the Quiet Centre

1 Come and find the qui - et cen - tre in the
2 Si - lence is a friend who claims us, cools the
3 In the Spir - it let us trav - el, op - en

crowd - ed life we lead, find the room for hope to
heat and slows the pace; God it is who speaks and
to each oth - er's pain, let our loves and fears un -

en - ter, find the frame where we are freed:
names us, knows our be - ing, face to face,
rav - el, cel - e - brate the space we gain:

Text: Shirley Erena Murray, 1992, alt. © 1992 Hope Publishing Co.
Music: Melody attrib. Benjamin Franklin White, 1844; harm. Ronald A. Nelson, 1978.
Harm. © 1978 Lutheran Book of Worship.

87 87D
BEACH SPRING

clear the cha - os and the clut - ter, clear our
mak - ing space with - in our think - ing, lift - ing
there's a place for deep - est dream - ing, there's a

eyes, that we can see all the things that real - ly
shades to show the sun, rais - ing cour - age when we're
time for heart to care, in the Spir - it's live - ly

mat - ter, be at peace, and sim - ply be.
shrink - ing, find - ing scope for faith be - gun.
schem - ing there is al - ways room to spare!

4   Everlasting God

Text and music: Brenton Brown and Ken Riley, 2005; arr. Ian Howarth.
© 2005 Thankyou Music; admin. EMI CMG Publishing.

Irregular
EVERLASTING GOD

Hallelujah! We Gather Here 5

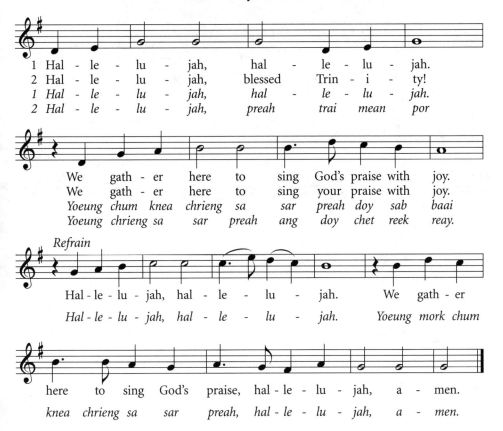

1 Hal - le - lu - jah, hal - le - lu - jah.
2 Hal - le - lu - jah, blessed Trin - i - ty!
1 *Hal - le - lu - jah, hal - le - lu - jah.*
2 *Hal - le - lu - jah, preah trai mean por*

We gath - er here to sing God's praise with joy.
We gath - er here to sing your praise with joy.
Yoeung chum knea chrieng sa sar preah doy sab baai
Yoeung chrieng sa sar preah ang doy chet reek reay.

Refrain

Hal - le - lu - jah, hal - le - lu - jah. We gath - er
Hal - le - lu - jah, hal - le - lu - jah. Yoeung mork chum

here to sing God's praise, hal - le - lu - jah, a - men.
knea chrieng sa sar preah, hal - le - lu - jah, a - men.

Text: Khmer text and music: Barnabas Mam, Cambodia, ©.
English text © 2000 General Board of Global Ministries.

810886

6 Ho, All Who Thirst

Refrain

Ho, all who thirst, come now to the wa-ter, and all whose souls are parched and wear-y, come and drink! Ho, all who thirst, come now to the wa-ter, and

Text and music: Alexander M. Peters, 1997, ©.

57 55 with refrain
JACOB'S WELL

from your heart will flow a nev - er - fail - ing spring!

G   Em   C   G   D   Gsus   G

1 Why for - sake the Lord, the fount of liv - ing wa - ter,
2 For the Lamb will be our shep - herd and will guide us
3 All who come may take this gift of liv - ing wa - ter.

Em   D   C   Em   D

to Refrain

choos - ing bro - ken cups that can - not be filled?
to the well - springs of the wa - ter of life.
They will thirst no more, for they shall be filled.

Em   F   Em   D   D7

7 Humbly in Your Sight

1 Hum - bly in your sight we come to - geth - er, Lord;
2 These, our hearts, are yours, we give them to you, Lord;
3 These, our eyes, are yours, we give them to you, Lord;
4 These, our hands, are yours, we give them to you, Lord;
5 These, our feet, are yours, we give them to you, Lord;

grant us now the bless - ing of your pres - ence here.
pur - i - fy our love to make it like your own.
may we al - ways see your world as with your sight.
give them strength and skill to do all work for you.
may we al - ways walk the path of life with you.

6 These, our tongues, are yours, we give them to you, Lord;
   may we speak your healing words of life and truth.

7 These, our ears, are yours, we give them to you, Lord;
   open them to hear the Gospel as from you.

8 Our whole selves are yours, we give them to you, Lord;
   take us now and keep us yours for evermore.

Text: Tumbuka text, J. P. Chirwa; trans. and adapt. Tom Colvin, 1967.
Music: Melody North Malawian trad.; adapt. Tom Colvin, 1967; arr. John L. Bell.
Text and music © 1967 Hope Publishing Co.

11 11
TIZA PANTAZI PINU

Let It Rise 8

1 Let the glo - ry of the Lord rise a - mong us. Let the
2 (Let the) songs of the Lord rise a - mong us. Let the

glo - ry of the Lord rise a - mong us. Let the
songs of the Lord rise a - mong us. Let the

prais - es of the King rise a - mong us. Let it rise.
joy of the King rise a - mong us. Let it rise.

1 Let the   2   Oh,

let it rise.   Oh,

let it rise.   (Let the)

Text and music: Holland Davis. © 1997 Maranatha Praise, Inc.

Irregular
LET IT RISE

9 I Rejoiced When I Heard Them Say

Text and music: Bernadette Farrell, 1993, ©; *admin. OCP Publications.*

LM with refrain
ENGLAND

10 Let Us Build a House

1 Let us build a house where love can dwell and all can safe - ly live, a place where saints and chil - dren tell how hearts learn to for - give. Built of

2 Let us build a house where proph - ets speak and words are strong and true, where all God's chil - dren dare to seek to dream God's reign a - new. Here the

3 Let us build a house where love is found in wa - ter, wine and wheat; a ban - quet hall on ho - ly ground, where peace and jus - tice meet. Here the

4 Let us build a house where hands will reach be - yond the wood and stone to heal and strength - en, serve and teach, and live the Word they've known. Here the

5 Let us build a house where all are named, their songs and vi - sions heard and loved and treas - ured, taught and claimed as words with - in the Word. Built of

Text and music: Marty Haugen, 1994. © 1994 GIA Publications, Inc.

96 86 87 10 with refrain
TWO OAKS

11 At Last We Gather Here Again/*Agnus Dei*

1 At last we gath - er here a - gain; you call to
2 Now we are safe be - hind your wings from all that
3 We bless the ban - quet you pre - pare from the rich
4 Your riv - er of de - lights is here, and we are
5 Here is the font that flows with life; you give us

O Lamb of God, you take a - way the sins

us, and we have come, at last, O God, at last.
seeks to do us harm; be - hind your wide - spread wings.
stores with - in your house: soon we will taste the feast.
thirs - ty; let us drink! A cup of joy, O God.
light and we can see, at last, O God, at last.

of the world: have mer - cy on us.
grant us your peace.

The Agnus Dei text is provided as an alternative
that may be used at the time of communion.

Text: Richard Leach, 2009. © 2009 Selah Publishing Co., Inc.
Music: David Buley, 2010. © 2010 Rublemusic Co.

886
AT LAST

God Welcomes All

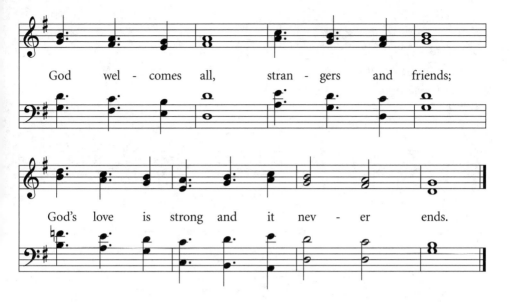

God wel - comes all, stran - gers and friends;

God's love is strong and it nev - er ends.

Text: John L. Bell, 2008.
Music: South African trad., transcr. John L. Bell, 2008.
Text and transc. © 2008 WGRG c/o Iona Community, GIA Publications, Inc., agent.

THEMBA AMEN

13 We Are All One People

Text: Lyrics by Joseph Naytowhow and Cheryl L'Hirondelle, 2000.
Music: Joseph Naytowhow, 2000. *Text and music © 2000 Miyoh Music, Inc.*

Irregular

14 Be Still and Know That I Am God

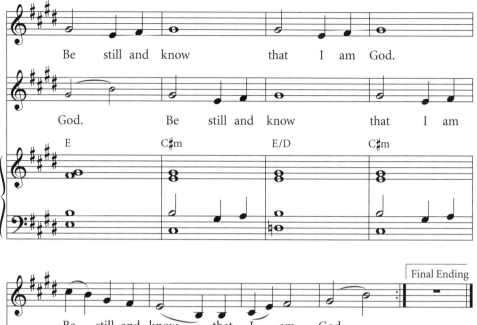

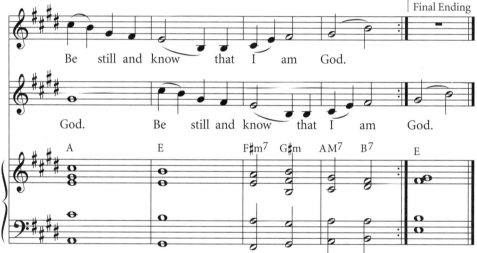

*Accompaniment is optional.

Text and music: John L. Bell, 1989. © 1989 WGRG c/o Iona Community, GIA Publications, Inc., agent. Irregular
PSALM 46

Jesu, tawa pano/Jesus, We Are Gathered   15

Je - su,   ta - wa   pa - no;   Je - su,
Je - sus,   we   are   gath - ered;   Je - sus,

ta - wa   pa - no;   Je - su,   ta - wa   pa - no;
we   are   gath - ered;   Je - sus,   we   are   gath - ered;

Leader: Mam - bo   Je - su.
O Lord Je - sus.

ta - wa   pa - no,   mu   zi - ta   re - nyu.
we   are   gath - ered,   to - geth - er   for   you.

Text and music: Patrick Matsikenyiri, 1990, ©.
Admin. General Board of Global Ministries t/a GBG Musik.

66 69
JESU, TAWA PANO

16 Come, All You People

Text: Alexander Gondo, 20th cent.; transcr. I-to Loh, 1986.
Music: Alexander Gondo, 20th cent.; arr. John L. Bell, 1994.
Arr. © 1994 WGRG c/o Iona Community, GIA Publications, Inc., agent.

56 56 56 7
UYAI MOSE

17 Lord, As I Wake I Turn to You

Unison

1 Lord, as I wake I turn to you, your-self the first
2 There is no bless-ing, Lord, from you for those who make
3 Your lov-ing gifts of grace to me, those fav-ours I
4 Lord, make my life a life of love; keep me from sin

thought of my day: my sov'-reign God, whose
their will their way, no praise for those who
could nev-er earn, call for my thanks in
in all I do; Lord, make your law my

help is sure, your-self the help for which I pray.
will not praise, no peace for those who will not pray.
praise and prayer, call me to love you in re-turn.
on-ly law, your will my will, for love of you.

Text: Ps. 5; para. Brian Foley, 1971, alt. © *1971 Faber Music Ltd.*
Music: Melody Irish trad.; harm. Martin Shaw. Harm. © *Oxford University Press.*

LM
DANIEL

1 Cre - a - tor, God, my gov - er - nor, my
2 I've been your ser - vant; still I serve and
3 You send me forth, each vow and prom - ise
4 You've brought sal - va - tion clear, de - liv - erance

guide, you give me leave at last to go to
will from birth un - til all a - ges end, and
kept, ac - cord - ing to the pro - phets' word. My
sure, to ev - ery na - tion, set - tled, wild, for

that great space where e - ven stars do hide their
then in peace and love will I serve still, nor
eyes, which searched so long, so of - ten wept, are
Is - rael's glo - ry— hope of rich and poor— is

1-3 | 4

fire in your more bril - liant glow.
cease when time it - self you rend.
o - pened now in joy as - sured.
God, em - bod - ied in a child.

Text: Sue Elwyn, SSJD, 2002.
Music: Adapt. from DRESDEN (*English Hymnal*); harm. J.S. Bach,
  by Thelma-Anne McLeod, SSJD, 2002. *Text and music © 2002 The Sisterhood of St. John the Divine.*

10 8 10 8
SEBASTIAN

19 Joyous Light of Heavenly Glory

1 Joy-ous light of heaven-ly glo - ry, lov-ing glow of God's own
2 In the stars that grace the dark - ness, in the blaz - ing sun of
3 You who made the heav-en's splen-dour, ev-ery danc-ing star of

face, you who sing cre - a - tion's sto - ry, shine on
dawn, in the light of peace and wis - dom we can
night, make us shine with gen - tle jus - tice, let us

ev - ery land and race. Now as eve - ning falls a -
hear your qui - et song. Love that fills the night with
each re - flect your light. Might-y God of all cre -

Text: Greek hymn, 3rd cent.; para. Marty Haugen, 1987.
Music: Marty Haugen, 1987.
Text and music © 1987 GIA Publications, Inc.

87 87D
JOYOUS LIGHT

round us   we shall raise   our songs to   you. God of   day - break,
won - der,   love that warms   the wear - y   soul,   love that bursts all
a - tion,   gen - tle Christ   who lights our   way,   lov - ing Spir - it

God   of   shad - ows,   come and   light our hearts   a - new.
chains a - sun - der,   set us   free and make   us   whole.
of   sal - va - tion,   lead us   on   to end - less   day.

20 My Prayers Rise Like Incense

Refrain Dm   Gm

My prayers rise like in - cense, my

Dm   Am7   Dm

hands like the eve - ning sac - ri - fice.

Verse

O Lord, I call to you; come to me quickly; hear my voice when I cry to you.

to Refrain

Set a watch be - fore my mouth, O Lord, and guard the door of my lips.

Text: Psalm 141; adapt. Arlo D. Duba, ©.
Music: Refrain Arlo D. Duba, arr. Geoff Weaver; verses John Harper.
Refrain © 1980 Arlo D. Duba; verses © 2000 The Royal School of Church Music.

Irregular

Verse 2

Let not my heart incline to a - ny e - vil thing;

let me not be occupied with e - vil do - ers.

But my eyes are turned to you, Lord God; in you I take refuge;

to Refrain

do not leave me de - fenceless.

When Twilight Comes and the Sun Sets

1 When twi-light comes and the sun sets, moth-er
2 One day the Rab-bi, Lord Je-sus, called the
3 So gath-er round once a-gain, friends, touched by

hen pre-pares for night's rest. As her brood shel-ters
twelve to share his last meal. As the hen tends her
fad-ing glow of sun's gold, and re-count all our

un-der her wings, she gives the love of God to her
young, so for them he spent him-self to seek and to
frail hu-man hopes, the dreams of young and sto-ries of

Text: Moises Andrade, 1990; trans. James Minchin, 1990,
    © admin. Asian Institute for Liturgy and Music.
Music: Francisco F. Feliciano, 1990, ©, admin. Asian Institute for Liturgy and Music;
    arr. Evangelical Lutheran Worship, 2006, © 2006 Augsburg Fortress.

88 99 97 77
DAPIT HAPON

22   Now That Evening Falls

1 Now that eve - ning falls, gen - tly fades the light;
2 Gra - ti - tude we raise for the day that's done
3 Glad - ly we com - mit to God's gra - cious care
4 Glo - ry be to God, glo - ry to God's son,

moon re - pla - ces sun and day takes leave of night.
and for what, to - mor - row, waits to be be - gun.
those we love and long for, those whose lives we share.
glo - ry to the Spir - it ev - er three in one.

Text and music: John L. Bell, 2002.

5 6 5 5
TAKING LEAVE

Child of Blessing, Child of Promise 23

1 Child of bless - ing, child of prom - ise, bap - tized with the Spir - it's sign, with this wa - ter God has sealed you un - to love and grace di - vine.

2 Child of love, our love's ex - pres - sion, love's cre - a - tion, love in - deed! Fresh from God, re - fresh our spir - its; in - to joy and laugh - ter lead.

3 Child of joy, our dear - est treas - ure, God's you are, from God you came. Back to God we hum - bly give you: live as one who bears Christ's name.

4 Child of God, your lov - ing Par - ent, learn to lis - ten for God's call. Grow to laugh and sing and wor - ship; trust and love God more than all.

Text: Ronald S. Cole-Turner, 1980, © 1981.
Music: Melody *Gross Catholisch Gesangbuch*, 1631. Arr. William Smith Rockstro.

87 87
OMNI DIE DIC MARIA

24 I Have Called You By Your Name

1 I have called you by your name, you are mine;
2 I will help you learn my name as you go;
3 I know you will need my touch as you go;
4 I have giv-en you a name, it is mine;

1 have gift-ed you and ask you now to shine.
read it writ-ten in my peo-ple, help them grow.
feel it puls-ing in cre-a-tion's ebb and flow.
I have giv-en you my Spir-it as a sign.

I will not a-ban-don you; all my prom-is-es are
Pour the wa-ter in my name, speak the word your soul can
Like the wom-an reach-ing out, choos-ing faith in spite of
With my won-der in your soul, make my wound-ed chil-dren

true. You are gift-ed, called, and chos-en; you are mine.
claim, of-fer Je-sus' bod-y, giv-en long a-go.
doubt, hold the hem of Je-sus' robe, then let it go.
whole; go and tell my pre-cious peo-ple they are mine.

Text and music: Daniel Charles Damon, 1989. © 1998 Hope Publishing Co.

10 11 7 7 11
KELLY

From the Waters of Creation 25

1 From the wa - ters of cre - a - tion to the shores of Gal - i - lee,
2 From the part - ing of the wa - ters to the Jor - dan's an - cient tide,
3 From the streams that A - mos vi - sioned to the pool where Je - sus healed,

in each riv - er sweep-ing on - ward there's a prom - ise we can see.
in the font, for - ev - er ris - ing, there's a love that will a - bide.
in the wells we build to - geth - er there's a dream that is re - vealed:

All who search for life in full - ness, all who long for dig - ni - ty:
All who yearn for gen - tle mer - cy, all who seek com - mu - ni - ty:
we will work for hope and jus - tice; we will live in un - i - ty.

come and drink now—don't be thirs - ty. God's grace ev - er will flow free.
come and wash now—don't be lone - ly. God's grace ev - er will flow free.
Come and share now—don't be fear - ful. God's grace ev - er will flow free.

Text: Keri K. Wehlander, 2007, ©.
Music: *A Repository of Sacred Music: Part Second*, Harrisburg, 1813.

87 87D
NETTLETON

26 Deep the Snows on God's High Mountain

Unison

1 Deep the snows on God's high moun - tain, bright and gleam - ing
2 E - den, land of lake and riv - er, ev - er pure and
3 Wells of old where shep - herds halt - ed, there to drink and
4 Zi - on's tem - ple saw God's glo - ry gush - ing forth from

in the sun. There set free, a liv - ing foun - tain stirs once
ev - er near. Grace and beau - ty sing to - geth - er, fresh the
find their rest, are by God a place ex - alt - ed: ris - ing
ev - ery door. Je - sus lives to be that sto - ry, time - less

more its course to run. Pool on pool by leaps de -
flow from year to year. Sing they too, her sons and
thirst is here ad - dressed. Came the Son true wealth pos -
fount on ev - ery shore. Wide the praise of throngs de -

scend - ing, brooks, now might - y tor - rents, roar. Shad - ed
daugh - ters, bathed and blest, so bright their soul. Gift of
ses - sing, large that heart to in - ter - cede. Liv - ing
clar - ing: his the life of love out - poured; he, the

Text: Peter Armour Niblock, 2015, ©.
Music: Melody Gaelic trad.; adapt. and arr. John L. Bell, 1989.
© 1989 WGRG c/o Iona Community, GIA Publications, Inc., agent.

87 87D
JESUS CALLS US
Alt. tune HYFRYDOL

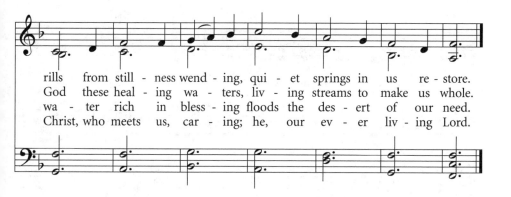

rills from still - ness wend - ing, qui - et springs in us re - store.
God these heal - ing wa - ters, liv - ing streams to make us whole.
wa - ter rich in bless - ing floods the des - ert of our need.
Christ, who meets us, car - ing; he, our ev - er liv - ing Lord.

You Have Put on Christ   27

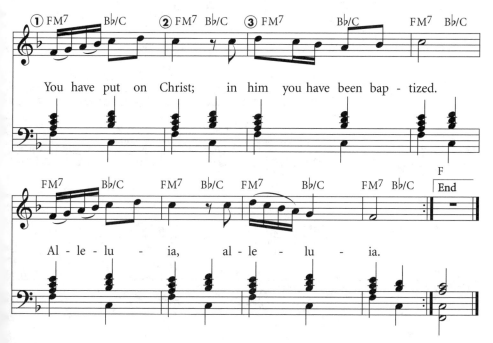

You have put on Christ; in him you have been bap - tized.

Al - le - lu - ia, al - le - lu - ia.

May be sung in two- or three-part canon; play chords only.

Text: ICEL, 1969.
Music: Howard Hughes, 1977.
Text © 1969 and music © 1977 International Commission on English in the Liturgy.

Irregular
BAPTIZED IN CHRIST

28 As I Went Down in the River to Pray

Lord, show me the way!

2. O brothers... 3. O fathers... 4. O mothers... 5. O sinners...

Text and music: American trad., arr. Michael Capon, 2008, ©.

Irregular
STARRY CROWN

God, When I Came into This Life

1 God, when I came in - to this life you called me by my name; to - day I come, com - mit my - self, re - spond - ing to your claim.

2 You give me free - dom to be - lieve; to - day I make my choice, and to the wor - ship of the church I add my learn - ing voice.

3 In all the ten - sions of my life, be - tween my faith and doubt, let your great Spir - it give me hope, sus - tain me, lead me out.

4 So help me in my un - be - lief and let my life be true: feet firm - ly plant - ed on the earth, my sights set high on you.

Text: Fred Kaan, 1976. © 1979 The Hymn Society, admin. Hope Publishing Co.
Music: Samuel McFarland, *The Beauties of Harmony*, 1813; arr. Kenneth Hull, 2019, ©.

CM
DUNLAP'S CREEK

30 All Who Hunger

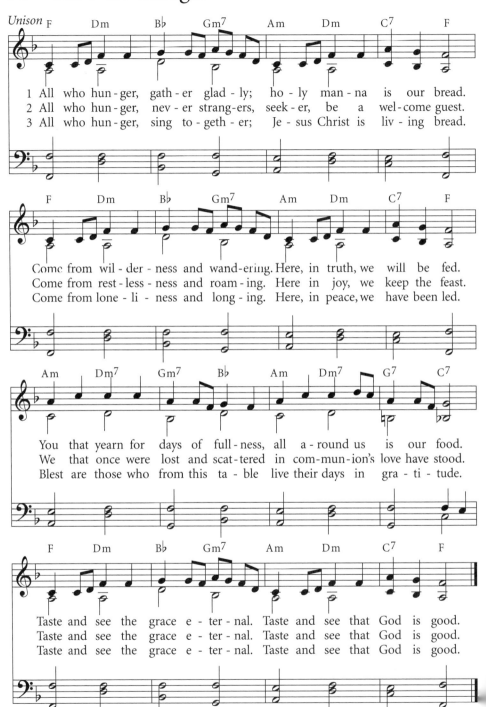

Unison

1 All who hun-ger, gath-er glad-ly; ho-ly man-na is our bread.
2 All who hun-ger, nev-er strang-ers, seek-er, be a wel-come guest.
3 All who hun-ger, sing to-geth-er; Je-sus Christ is liv-ing bread.

Come from wil-der-ness and wand-ering. Here, in truth, we will be fed.
Come from rest-less-ness and roam-ing. Here in joy, we keep the feast.
Come from lone-li-ness and long-ing. Here, in peace, we have been led.

You that yearn for days of full-ness, all a-round us is our food.
We that once were lost and scat-tered in com-mun-ion's love have stood.
Blest are those who from this ta-ble live their days in gra-ti-tude.

Taste and see the grace e-ter-nal. Taste and see that God is good.
Taste and see the grace e-ter-nal. Taste and see that God is good.
Taste and see the grace e-ter-nal. Taste and see that God is good.

Text: Sylvia G. Dunstan, 1991. © 1991 GIA Publications, Inc.
Music: Attr. William Moore, 1825; arr. Michael Capon, 2016, ©.

87 87D
HOLY MANNA

Beyond the Beauty and the Awe

1 Be - yond the beau - ty and the awe, be -
2 Our lives feel torn be - tween the world whose
3 Oh, teach us how to hear your voice de -
4 In sound or si - lence, sight or smell, may
5 Then help us live as Je - sus taught, as

yond the fear and dread, we long, O God, to
needs are grim - ly real and emp - ty talk of
spite the traf - fic's din; to keep the blasts of
we some to - ken find that makes your liv - ing
light and salt and yeast, that oth - ers may be

hear your word, to taste your trans - formed bread.
peace and joy with dis - tant, vague ap - peal.
ran - cour out and let your Spir - it in.
pres - ence known to bod - y, soul, and mind.
brought to share your prom - ise and your feast.

Text: Carl P. Daw, Jr., 1994. © 1994 Hope Publishing Co.   CM
Music: Melody *Sixteen Tune Settings*, Philadelphia, 1812; harm. C. Winfred Douglas, 1940. MORNING SONG

32 When at This Table

Capo 1

1 When at this ta - ble I re - ceive a bless - ing,
2 If at this ta - ble I have need of heal - ing,
3 If at this ta - ble I for - get the hun - gry,
4 If at this ta - ble I make ded - i - ca - tion
5 What faith I have I bring to join this ta - ble;

the bro - ken bread, the wine of life for me,
un - bid - den grief, re - la - tion - ship gone wrong,
the dis - pos - sessed, and war - fare's spread - ing stain,
to give my life in serv - ing what is good,
what hope I hold, in Christ is taught and true.

then let me share the peace with you, my neigh - bour,
then let me know the hands of God en - fold - ing,
then let this bread be - come the bread of judge - ment,
then let my cen - tre be where God in - vites me,
With broth - ers, sis - ters, I will share the bless - ing,

Text: Shirley Erena Murray, 2004.
Music: Jane Marshall, 2005. *Text © 2004 and music © 2005 Hope Publishing Co.*

11 10 11 10
FEASTDAY

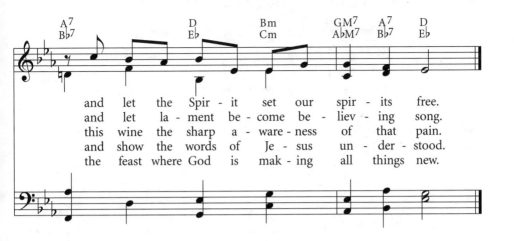

and let the Spir - it set our spir - its free.
and let la - ment be - come be - liev - ing song.
this wine the sharp a - ware - ness of that pain.
and show the words of Je - sus un - der - stood.
the feast where God is mak - ing all things new.

Now in This Banquet

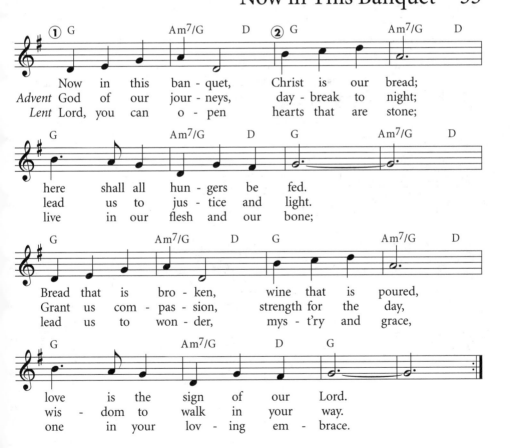

Now in this ban - quet, Christ is our bread;
Advent God of our jour - neys, day - break to night;
Lent Lord, you can o - pen hearts that are stone;

here shall all hun - gers be fed.
lead us to jus - tice and light.
live in our flesh and our bone;

Bread that is bro - ken, wine that is poured,
Grant us com - pas - sion, strength for the day,
lead us to won - der, mys - t'ry and grace,

love is the sign of our Lord.
wis - dom to walk in your way.
one in your lov - ing em - brace.

May be sung in canon.

Text and music: Marty Haugen, 1986. © 1986 GIA Publications, Inc.

34 We Will Take What You Offer

We will take what you of-fer, we will live by your word; we will
We will, we will live by your word;

love one an-oth-er and be fed by you, Lord. We will
we will be fed by you, Lord.

take what you of-fer, we will live by your word; we will
We will, we will live by your word;

love one an-oth-er and be fed by you, Lord.
we will be fed by you, Lord.

Text and music: John L. Bell, 1998.
© 1998 WGRG c/o Iona Community, GIA Publications, Inc., agent.

76 76D

Hope Is a Star 35

1 Hope is a star that shines in the night,
2 Peace is a rib-bon that cir - cles the earth,
3 Joy is a song that wel - comes the dawn,
4 Love is a flame that burns in our heart.

lead - ing us on till the morn - ing is bright.
giv - ing a prom - ise of safe - ty and worth.
tell - ing the world that the Sav - iour is born.
Je - sus has come and will nev - er de - part.

Refrain

When God is a child there's joy in our song. The last shall be first and the weak shall be strong, and none shall be a - fraid.

Text: Brian Wren, 1985.
Music: Joan Collier Fogg, 1987. *Text and music © 1989 Hope Publishing Co.*

Irregular with refrain
MOON BEAMS

36 O Ancient Love

Unison

1 O an-cient love, pro-cess-ing through the a-ges;
2 O home-less love, that dwells a-mong the stran-ger;
3 O gen-tle love, ca-ress-ing those in sor-row;
4 O suf-fering love, that bears our hu-man weak-ness;

O hid-den love, re-vealed in hu-man form;
O low-ly love, that knows the might-y's scorn;
O ten-der love, that com-forts those for-lorn;
O bound-less love, that ris-es with the morn;

O prom-ised love, the dream of seers and sa-ges:
O hun-gry love, that lay with-in the man-ger:
O hope-ful love, that prom-is-es to-mor-row:
O might-y love, con-cealed in in-fant meek-ness:

Text and music: Michael Joncas, 1994. © 1994 GIA Publications, Inc.

11 10 11 10 10
BEDFORD ABBEY

O liv-ing Love, with-in our hearts be born;

O liv-ing Love, with-in our hearts be borne.

Give Us Light/*Jyothi dho Prabhu*   37

1	Give	us	light;	give	us	light;	give	us	light,	O Lord.
2	Give	us	life;	give	us	life;	give	us	life,	O Lord.
3	Grant	us	peace;	grant	us	peace;	grant	us	peace,	O Lord.
4	Save	us	now;	save	us	now;	save	us	now,	O Lord.
5	Give	us	grace;	give	us	grace;	give	us	grace,	O Lord.

Hindi

1 *Jyothi dho Prabhu.*
2 *Jiivan dho Prabhu.*
3 *Shanthi dho Prabhu.*
4 *Mukthi dho Prabhu.*
5 *Aasish dho Prabhhu.*

Text and music: Charles Vas, 1990.
© 1990 Christian Conference of Asia; admin. GIA Publications, Inc.   JYOTHI DHO

38 Wild and Lone the Prophet's Voice

1 Wild and lone the proph-et's voice ech-oes through the des-ert still, call-ing us to make a choice, bid-ding us to do God's will: "Turn from

2 "Bear the fruit re-pen-tance sows: lives of jus-tice, truth, and love. Trust no oth-er claim than those; set your heart on things a-bove. Soon the

3 With such preach-ing stark and bold John pro-claimed sal-va-tion near, and his time-less warn-ings hold words of hope to all who hear. So we

Text: Carl P. Daw, Jr., 1989. © 1989 Hope Publishing Co.
Music: David Ashley White, 1996. © 1996 Selah Publishing Co., Inc.

77 77 D
LA GRANGE

39 Stay Awake, Be Ready

Text and music: Christopher Walker, 1988. © 1988 Christopher Walker, admin. OCP Publications.

Irregular
STAY AWAKE

No Wind At the Window   40

1 No wind at the win-dow, no knock on the door;
2 "O Mar-y, O Mar-y, don't hide from my face.
3 "This child must be born that the king-dom might come:
4 No pay-ment was prom-ised, no prom-is-es made;

no light from the lamp-stand, no foot on the floor;
Be glad that you're fav-oured and filled with God's grace.
sal - va-tion for man-y, de-struc-tion for some;
no wed-ding was dat-ed, no blue-print dis - played.

no dream born of tired-ness, no ghost raised by fear:
The time for re - deem-ing the world has be - gun,
both end and be - gin-ning, both mes-sage and sign;
Yet Mar - y, con - sent-ing to what none could guess,

just an an - gel and a wom - an and a voice in her ear.
and you are re - quest-ed to moth - er God's Son."
both vic - tor and vic - tim, both yours and di - vine."
re - plied with con - vic - tion, "Tell God I say 'Yes.'"

Text: John L. Bell, 1992.
Music: Melody Irish trad.; arr. John L. Bell, 1992.
Text and arr. © 1992 WGRG c/o Iona Community, GIA Publications, Inc., agent.

11 11 11 11
COLUMCILLE

41 Come, Come Emmanuel

(come.)

Last time to final ending

All

Come, come Emmanuel. Come, Em-

G D/F# Cadd2/E Bm/D C

Cantor

1 For the Lord of cre-a-tion will
2 Oh, the son of Mar-y will
3 See God's mar-vel-lous deeds and
4 For God chose us, and so we will
5 For the an-gel pro-claims he will
6 As the ser-vants of God we

Lord, have mer-cy up-on us and
Christ, have mer-cy up-on us and
Lord, have mer-cy up-on us and

This chant works well with or without the cantor's part. There are two independent sets of words for a cantor: vs. 1–6 are words for Advent or times of invocation; the words for the "Kyrie" below are prayers of confession and similar confessions.

Final ending

man - u - el. man - u - el.

Dsus4 D7 Em C6 Dsus4 D7 Cadd2 C G

Text and music: James J. Chepponis, 1995. © 1995 GIA Publications, Inc.

65

COME, COME EMMANUEL

What Shall We Give to the Child 42

Text: Stephen Dean, 1995.
Music: Catalan trad., arr. Stephen Dean, 1995.
Text and arr. © 1995 Stephen Dean. Published by OCP Publications.

11 10 11 10
CATALAN CAROL

43 Holy Child within the Manger

Capo 1

1 Ho - ly child with - in the man - ger, long a -
2 Once a - gain we tell the sto - ry— how your
3 Ho - ly child with - in the man - ger, lead us

go yet ev - er near; come as friend to ev - ery
love for us was shown, when the im - age of your
ev - er in your way, so we see in ev - ery

stran - ger, come as hope for ev - ery fear. As you
glo - ry wore an im - age like our own. Come, en -
stran - ger how you come to us to - day. In our

Text and music: Marty Haugen, 1987. © 1987 GIA Publications, Inc.

87 87D
JOYOUS LIGHT

44 There Were Angels Hov'ring Round

1 There were an - gels hov' - ring round, there were an - gels hov' - ring round, there were an - gels, an - gels hov' - ring round!
2 They sing in har - mo - ny, they sing in har - mo - ny, they sing, they sing in har - mo - ny.
3 The child in her arms, the child in her arms, the child, the child in her arms.
4 The shep - herds on their knees, the shep - herds on their knees, the shep - shep - herds on their knees.
5 There are an - gels hov' - ring round, there are an - gels hov' - ring round, there are an - gels, an - gels hov' - ring round!

More verses may be added to fill out the story.

Text and music: American trad.

Today I Live 45

Unison

1 To - day I live, one day shall come my
2 How I shall die, or when, I do not
3 When earth - ly life shall close, as close it
4 Mean - while I live and move and I am

death; one day shall still my laugh - ter and my
know, nor where, for end - less is the world's hor -
must, let Je - sus be my broth - er and my
glad, en - joy this life and all its in - ter -

cry - ing, bring to a halt my heart - beat and my
i - zon; but save me, God, from thoughts that lay me
mer - it. Let me with - out re - gret re - call the
weav - ings; each giv - en day, as I take up the

breath: oh, give me faith for liv - ing and for dy - ing.
low, from mor - bid fears that freeze my power of rea - son.
past, and then in - to your hands com - mit my spir - it.
thread, let love sug - gest my mode, my mood of liv - ing.

Text: Fred Kaan, 1975. © 1975 Hope Publishing Co.
Music: Margaret R. Tucker, 1998. © 1998 Hope Publishing Co.

10 11 10 11
ROBERT

46 Jesus, Tempted in the Desert

1 Je - sus, tempt - ed in the des - ert, lone - ly, hun - gry,
2 Je - sus, tempt - ed at the tem - ple, high a - bove its
3 Je - sus, tempt - ed on the moun - tain by the lure of
4 When we face temp - ta - tion's pow - er, lone - ly, strug - gling,

filled with dread: "Use your power," the tempt - er tells him;
an - cient wall: "Throw your - self from loft - y tur - ret;
vast do - main: "Fall be - fore me! Be my ser - vant!
filled with dread, Christ, who knew the tempt - er's hour,

"turn these bar - ren rocks to bread!" "Not a - lone by bread," he
an - gels wait to break your fall!" Je - sus shuns such emp - ty
Glo - ry, fame, you're sure to gain!" Je - sus sees the daz - zling
come and be our liv - ing bread. By your grace pro - tect, pre -

Text: Herman G. Stuempfle, 1993. © 1993, GIA Publications, Inc.
Music: Thomas John Williams, 1890.

87 87D
EBENEZER

an - swers, "can the hu - man heart be filled. On - ly by the
mar - vels, feats that fick - le crowds re - quest: "God, whose grace pro -
vi - sion, turns his eyes an - oth - er way: "God a - lone de -
serve us, lest we fall, your trust be - tray. Yours, a - bove all

Word that calls us is our deep - est hun - ger stilled!"
tects, pre - serves us, we must nev - er vain - ly test."
serves our hom - age! God a - lone will I o - bey."
oth - er voic - es, be the Word we hear, o - bey.

47 So Much Wrong

Unison

1 So much wrong and so much in-jus - tice, so you
2 Ol - ive trees showed the pain of sor - row; they were
3 No fine song, no im-press-ive mu - sic can at -
4 Ev - ery - thing I could ev-er of - fer could not

shoul - dered a wood-en cross. Now like you my best dreams are
griev - ing for their Lord. Round Je - ru - sa-lem the hills were
tempt to re-lieve my heart; in this hour I am called to
pay for what God has done; but my life shall be spent in

shat - tered; all I know is the weight of loss.
mourn - ing as the ci - ty de - nied its God. My be -
griev - ing lest no oth - er will play this part.
hon - our of my Sav - iour, God's on - ly Son.

lov - ed, my be - lov - ed, tell me, where can you be found? You drank

Text: Arabic; Eng. version John L. Bell, 2005.
Music: 16th cent. French melody; adapt. John L. Bell, 2005.
Text and music © 2005 WGRG c/o Iona Community, GIA Publications, Inc., agent.

98 98 with refrain
SO MUCH WRONG

deep of the cup of suf - fer-ing, and your death is our ho - ly ground.

Eternal Christ You Rule 48

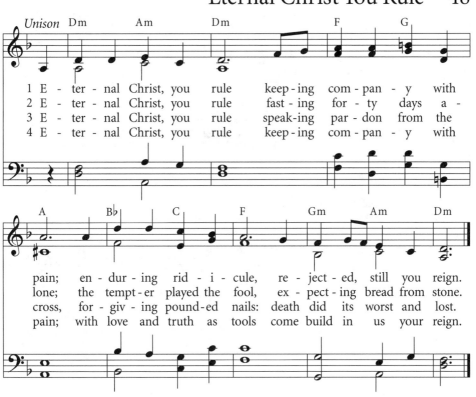

Unison Dm   Am   Dm   F   G

1 E - ter - nal Christ, you rule   keep-ing com - pan - y with
2 E - ter - nal Christ, you rule   fast - ing for - ty days a -
3 E - ter - nal Christ, you rule   speak-ing par - don from the
4 E - ter - nal Christ, you rule   keep-ing com - pan - y with

A   Bb   C   F   Gm   Am   Dm

pain; en - dur - ing rid - i - cule, re - ject - ed, still you reign.
lone; the tempt - er played the fool, ex - pect - ing bread from stone.
cross, for - giv - ing pound-ed nails: death did its worst and lost.
pain; with love and truth as tools come build in us your reign.

Text and music: Daniel Charles Damon, 1990, rev. 2010. © 1991 Hope Publishing Co.

67 66
THROCKMORTON

49 Lord, Why Have You Forsaken Me

1 Lord, why have you for - sak - en me and
2 Yet you are ho - ly, and the songs of
3 But I am mocked and put to scorn. All
4 Yet you, O Lord, have been my God and

why are you so far a - way from my com-plaint and
praise of Is - rael are your throne; when our an - ces - tors
those who see me laugh and say, "You trust in God, so
on - ly hope since I was born. With trou - ble near me,

my dis - tress poured out be - fore you night and day?
called on you, you saved them, res - cued all your own.
let us see the help of God to whom you pray."
none can help; my Sav - iour, leave me not for - lorn.

Text: Christopher L. Webber, 1986, ©.
Music: Walker's *Southern Harmony*, 1835.

LM
DISTRESS

"Why Has God Forsaken Me?" 50

Unison

1 "Why has God for - sak - en me?" Je - sus cried out
2 At the tomb of Laz - a - rus Je - sus wept with
3 Je - sus, as his life ex - pired, placed him - self with -
4 Mys - tery shrouds our life and death but we need not

from the cross as he shared the lone - li - ness
o - pen grief: grant us, God, the tears which heal
in God's care: at our dy - ing, Christ, may we
be a - fraid, for the mys - tery's heart is love,

of our deep - est grief and loss.
all our pain and un - be - lief.
trust the love which con - quers fear.
God's great love which Christ dis - played.

Text: William L. Wallace, 1980. © 1993 Selah Publishing Co., Inc.
Music: Taihei Sato, 1981. © 1983 Christian Conference of Asia, admin. GIA Publications, Inc.

77 77
SHIMPI

51 Senzeni ma

Leader

Sen - ze - ni na?

All

Sen - ze - ni na? Sen - ze - ni

Sen - ze - ni na?

na? Sen - ze - ni na? Sen - ze - ni

Sen - ze - ni na? Sen - ze - ni na?

na? Sen - ze - ni na? Sen - ze - ni na?

Sen - ze - ni na?

Sen - ze - ni na? Sen - ze - ni na?

Zulu pronunciation: Sehn-zeh-nee han.
Translation: "What have we done?"

Text and Music: South African trad.; arr. *More Voices*, 2007.
Arr. © 2007 The United Church of Canada.

 SENZENI NA

Crucem tuam/O Lord, Your Cross 52

Cru - cem tu - am a - do - ra - mus Do - mi -
O Lord, your cross we a - dore and glo - ri -

ne. Re - sur - rec - ti - o - nem tu - am lau - da - mus Do - mi -
fy. For your ho - ly res - ur - rec - tion we praise you, Lord of

ne. Lau - da - mus et glo - ri - fi - ca - mus.
life. We praise you and we glo - ri - fy you.

Re - sur - rec - ti - o - nem tu - am lau - da - mus Do - mi - ne.
For your ho - ly res - ur - rec - tion we praise you, Lord of life.

Text: Taizé Community, 1991.
Music: Jacques Berthier, 1991.
Text and music © 1991 Les Presses de Taizé; admin. GIA Publications, Inc.

CRUCEM TUAM

53 Christ Has Arisen/*Mfurahini, haleluya*

M - fu - ra - hi - ni, ha - le - lu - ya, m - ko - mbo-
1 Christ has a - ris - en, al - le - lu - ia. Re - joice and
2 For three long days the grave did its worst un - til its
3 The an - gel said to them, "Do not fear. You look for

zi a - me - fu - fu - ka. A - me - fu - fu - ka,
praise him, al - le - lu - ia. For our re - deem - er
strength by God was dis - persed. He who gives life did
Je - sus who is not here. See for your - selves, the

ha - le - lu - ya, m - si - fu - ni sa - sa ya ha - i.
burst from the tomb, ev - en from death, dis - pell - ing its gloom.
death un - der - go, and in its con - quest his might did show.
tomb is all bare. On - ly the grave clothes are ly - ing there."

4 "Go spread the news: he's not in the grave.
He has arisen this world to save.
Jesus' redeeming labours are done.
Even the battle with sin is won."

5 Christ has arisen to set us free.
Alleluia, to him praises be.
Jesus is living! Let us all sing;
he reigns triumphant, heavenly king.

Text: Bernard Kyamanywa, 1968. English trans. Howard S. Olson, 1977.
Text © 1968 Lutheran Theological College, Makomira, Tanzania;
admin. Augsburg Fortress. Eng. trans. © 1977 Augsburg Fortress.
Music: Tanzanian trad.

99 99 with refrain
MFURAHINI, HALELUYA

Tu - mwi - mbi - e   so - te   kwa   fu - ra - ha.   Ye - su   a -
Let   us   sing   praise   to   him   with   end - less   joy.   Death's fear - ful

me - to - ka   ka - bu - ri - ni.   Ka - shi - nda   ki - fo,
sting   he   has   come   to   des - troy.   Our   sin   for - giv - ing,

ha - le - lu - ya;   ha - le - lu - ya,   Ye - su   ya   ha - i.
al - le - lu - ia!   Je - sus   is   liv - ing,   al - le - lu - ia!

54 ¡Resucitó!

Refrain

Am
¡Re - su - ci - tó!
¡A - le - lu - ya!

¡Re - su - ci - tó!
¡A - le - lu - ya!

G
¡Re - su - ci -
¡A - le - lu -

F
tó!
ya!

¡A - le - lu - ya!
¡Re - su - ci - tó!

E

Final ending
E   Am
¡Re - su - ci - tó!

Am
1 Je - su - cris - to   ya ven - ció la
2 ¿Dón - de, oh muer - te,   dón - de es - tá tu
1 And   death now,   van - ished is the
2 The   king - dom, praise to God, the

Text and music: Kiko Arüello; tr. Robert C. Trupia, siglo XX;
Music arr. Philip W. Blycker, ©. *Text and music © 1972, 1988, Francisco (Kiko) Gómez
Argüello y Editiones Musical PAX-PPC. Admin. OCP Publications.*

6 66 with refrain
RESUCITÓ

muer - te;　　　con po - der glo - rio - so
triun - fo?　　　¿Dón - de, oh se - pul - cro,
fear now,　　　ban - ished are my tears now,
king - dom!　　　Raised up to the king - dom,

ha re - su - ci - ta - do.
dón - de tu vic - to - ria?
death has passed a - way.
we shall live in love.

D.C. al Fine

Español　3　El promete, que también nosotros
　　　　　　resucitaremos. ¡Gloria, aleluya!

　　　　　4　¡Alegría, alegría fieles!
　　　　　　¡Jesucristo vive; ha resucitado!

English　3　Our gladness, blissful in our gladness,
　　　　　　this will be our gladness, that he is alive.

　　　　　4　With him then, die and live with him then,
　　　　　　rise and sing our hymn then, sing alleluia.

55 Our Wars and Tumults Now Must Cease

1 Our wars and tu - mults now must cease:
2 From death's grim har - vest and de - cree
3 By your deep wounds, O Je - sus bring
4 Christ closed the gates of hell and fear;
5 Christ rose the third day to pro - claim

vic - tor - ious life and love and peace
Je - sus' a - ris - ing sets us free.
your peo - ple freed from death's dread sting,
be - hold! now heav'n's wide halls ap - pear!
heav'n's life's for all, for all to claim.

al - read - y reign! Let joy in - crease!
Now earth joins heav - en's har - mo - ny:
that we may ev - er live to sing: Al - le - lu - ia!
Re - joice and sing for all to hear:
Let peo - ple shout this great re - frain:

Text: *Finita jam sunt praelia*, 1695; tr. William Whitla, 2005, ©.
Music: Giovanni Pierluigi da Palestrina, 1591; adapt. William Henry Monk, 1861.

888 with Alleluias
VICTORY
Alt. tune VULPIUS

Come, Join the Dance of Trinity   56

1 Come, join the dance of Trin-i-ty, be-fore all worlds be-gun—
2 Come, see the face of Trin-i-ty, new-born in Beth-le-hem;
3 Come, speak a-loud of Trin-i-ty, as wind and tongues of flame
4 With-in the dance of Trin-i-ty, be-fore all worlds be-gun,

the in-ter-weav-ing of the Three, the Fa-ther, Spir-it, Son.
then blood-ied by a crown of thorns out-side Je-ru-sa-lem.
set peo-ple free at Pen-te-cost to tell the Sav-iour's name.
we sing the prais-es of the Three, the Fa-ther, Spir-it, Son.

The u-ni-verse of space and time did not a-rise by chance,
The dance of Trin-i-ty is meant for hu-man flesh and bone;
We know the yoke of sin and death, our necks have worn it smooth;
Let voic-es rise and in-ter-weave, by love and hope set free,

but as the Three, in love and hope, made room with-in their dance.
when fear con-fines the dance in death, God rolls a-way the stone.
go tell the world of weight and woe that we are free to move!
to shape in song this joy, this life: the dance of Trin-i-ty.

Text: Richard Leach, 2001. © 2001 Selah Publishing Co.
Music: Melody English trad.; adapt. and harm. Ralph Vaughan Williams, 1906.
    Harm. © Oxford University Press.

MD
KINGSFOLD

57 O Threefold God of Tender Unity

1 O three - fold God of ten - der u - ni - ty,
2 O blaze of ra - diance, source of light that blinds,
3 In ev - ery mak - ing, each cre - a - tive dream,
4 O three - fold God of ten - der u - ni - ty,

life's great un - known that binds and sets us free:
fierce burn - ing fire in clear pro - phet - ic minds,
and in the flow - ing of life's heal - ing stream,
life's great un - known that binds and sets us free:

Text: William L. Wallace, 2005.
Music: Gaelic melody, transcr. Alasdair Codona; harm. Alfred V. Fedak, 2020.
Text © 2008 and harm. © 2021 Selah Publishing Co., Inc.

10 10 10 10
AZAIR
Alt. tune SURSUM CORDA

felt   in   our   lov - ing,   great - er   than   our   thought,
you   live   in   mys - tery,   yet   with - in   us   dwell;
when love   is   born   or   peo - ple   re - con - ciled,
felt   in   our   lov - ing,   great - er   than   our   thought,

you   are   the   mys - tery   found,   the   mys - tery   sought.
life   springs from you   as   from   a   liv - ing   well.
we   share   your   life,   O   Par - ent, Spir - it,   Child.
you   are   the   mys - tery   found,   the   mys - tery   sought.

58 Mothering God

1 Moth - er - ing God, you gave me birth in the bright morn-ing of this world. Cre - a - tor, source of ev - ery breath, you are my rain, my wind, my sun.

2 Moth - er - ing Christ, you took my form, of - fer - ing me your food of light, grain of life, and grape of love, your ver - y bod - y for my peace.

3 Moth - er - ing Spir - it, nur - tur-ing one, in arms of pa - tience hold me close so that in faith I root and grow un - til I flower, un - til I know.

Text: Jean Janzen, 1991, ©; adapt. from Julian of Norwich.
Music: Michael Capon, 2016, ©.

LM

Those Hearts that We Have Treasured 59

1 Those hearts that we have trea - sured, those lives that
2 They still give hope and com - fort, they did not
3 From hearts that we have trea - sured, from lives that

we have shared, those loves that walked be - side
lose the fight, they showed us truth and good -
we have shared, from loves that walked be - side

us, those friends for whom we've cared— their bless - ing
ness, they shine in - to our night. Re - mem - ber
us, from friends for whom we've cared, we've learned to

rests up - on us, their life is mem - o -
days of glad - ness, re - mem - ber times of
trea - sure kind - ness, we've learned that grace pro -

Text: Sylvia G. Dunstan, 1991. © 1991 GIA Publications, Inc.
Music: Melody The Southern Harmony, 1835; harm. Dale Grotenhuis, ©.

76 76D
RESIGNATION

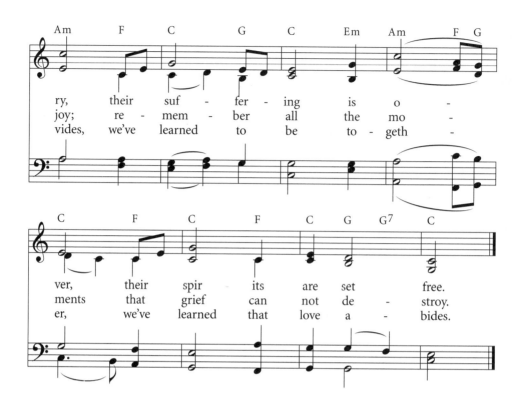

ry,   their suf -   fer - ing   is   o   -
joy;   re - mem -   ber   all   the   mo   -
vides,   we've learned   to   be   to - geth -

ver,   their   spir   its   are   set   free.
ments   that   grief   can   not de -   stroy.
er,   we've learned that   love   a -   bides.

These Are the Days of Elijah   60

1 These are the days of E - li - jah de -
clar - ing the Word of the Lord; and
these are the days of your ser - vant Mo - ses,
right - eous - ness be - ing re - stored. And
though these are days of great tri - als,
fam - ine and dark - ness and sword, still
we are the voice in the des - ert cry - ing, "Pre -
pare ye the way of the Lord." Be - hold He

2 these are the days of E - ze - kiel, the
dry bones be - com - ing as flesh; and
these are the days of your ser - vant Da - vid, re -
build - ing a tem - ple of praise. And
these are the days of the har - vest—the
fields are as white in the world; and
we are the la - bour - ers in your vine - yard, de -
clar - ing the Word of the Lord.

Text and music: Robin Mark, 1996.
© 1996 Daybreak Music; admin. Integrity's Hosanna! Music (ASCAP).

Irregular
DAYS OF ELIJAH

Hey! Be-hold He comes, rid-ing on the clouds,

shin-ing like the sun at the trum-pet

call. Lift your voice, it's the year of Ju-bi-lee,

and out of Zi-on's hill sal - va - tion

comes. Be - hold, he comes.

61 Lord of Life, We Come to You

Unison

1 Lord of life, we come to you. Lord of all, our Sav-iour be, come to bless and to heal with the light of your love.

2 Through the days of doubt and toil, in our joy and in our pain, guide our steps in your way, make us one in your love.

Text: Catherine Walker, 1998. © *St Mungo Music, Presbytery of St Leo the Great, Glasgow.*
Music: Melody Scottish trad.; arr. Alfred V. Fedak. © *2020 Selah Publishing Co., Inc.*

77 66
ERISKAY LOVE LILT

When We Must Bear Persistent Pain

1 When we must bear per - sis - tent pain and
2 Sup - port us as we learn new ways to
3 We thank you for the bet - ter days when
4 In ease or pain, in life and death, to

suf - fer with no cure in sight, come,
care for bod - ies new - ly frail. Help
we may smile to greet the sun, to
you our frag - ile lives be - long, and

Ho - ly Pres - ence, breathe your peace with
us en - dure, and live and love. Hear
do your work with clear - ing mind, and
so we trust you in all things. You

gifts of warmth and heal - ing light.
our com - plaint when pa - tience fails.
bless your name when day is done.
are our hope, our health, our song.

Text: Ruth Duck, 2004. © 2005 GIA Publications, Inc.
Music: William Walker's *Southern Harmony*, 1835; harm. David N. Johnson, 1968.
  Harm. © 1968 Augsburg Fortress.

LM
PROSPECT

63 God Weeps with Us Who Weep and Mourn

1 God weeps with us who weep and mourn; God's
tears flow down with ours, and God's own heart is
bruised and worn from all the heav-y hours of

2 Through tears and sor-row, God, we share a
sense of your vast grief: the weight of bear-ing
ev-ery prayer for heal-ing and re-lief, the

3 And yet be-cause, like us, you weep, we
trust you will re-ceive and in your ten-der
heart will keep the ones for whom we grieve, while

Text: Thomas H. Troeger, 1996, alt. © 2002 Oxford University Press.
Music: Sally Ann Morris, 1995. © 1998 GIA Publications, Inc.

CMD
MOSHIER

watch - ing while the soul's bright fire burned
bur - den of our ques - tions why, the
with your tears our hearts will taste the

low - er day by day, and pulse and breath and
doubts that they en - gage, and as our friends and
deep, dear core of things from which both life and

love's de - sire dimmed down to ash and clay.
loved ones die, our hope - less - ness and rage.
death are graced by love's re - new - ing springs.

Last stanza only

64 Go, Silent Friend

1 Go, si - lent friend, your life has found its end - ing; to dust re-
2 Go, si - lent friend, for - give us if we grieved you; safe now in

turns your wear - y mor - tal frame. God, who be-
heav - en, kind - ly say our name. Your life has

fore birth called you in - to be - ing, now calls you
touched us, that is why we mourn you; our lives with-

hence, his ac - cent still the same. Go, si - lent
out you can - not be the same. Go, si - lent

Text: John L. Bell, 1996. © 1996 WGRG c/o Iona Community, GIA Publications, Inc., agent.
Music: Melody Irish trad., arr. Frederick C. Silvester, 1938, alt.

11 10 11 10D
LONDONDERRY AIR

friend,   your   life   in   Christ is   bur - ied;   for   you   he
friend,   we   do   not grudge you glo - ry;   sing, sing with

lived   and died and rose a - gain.   Close by   his
joy   deep prais - es to your Lord.   You, who be -

side   your prom - ised place is   wait - ing,   where, ful - ly
lieved   that Christ would come back for   you,   now cel - e -

known, you   shall with God   re -   main.
brate   that Je - sus keeps   his   word.

As an alternative to singing, the text may be read by a single voice while the music is played.

65 We Cannot Care for You the Way We Wanted

1 We can - not care for you the way we want - ed, or
2 We can - not watch you grow - ing in - to child - hood and
3 We can - not know the pain or the po - ten - tial which
4 So through the mess of an - ger, grief, and tired - ness, through
5 Lord, in your arms, which cra - dle all cre - a - tion, we

cra - dle you or lis - ten for your cry; but,
find a new u - nique - ness ev - ery day; but
pass - ing years would sum - mon or re - veal; but
ten - sions which are not yet re - con - ciled, we
rest and place our ba - by be - yond death, be -

sep - a - rat - ed as we are by si - lence,
spe - cial as you would have been a - mong us,
for that true ful - fill - ment Je - sus prom - ised
give to God the wor - ship of our sor - row
liev - ing that *s/he* now, a - live in heav - en,

Text and music: John L. Bell, 1996.
© 1996 WGRG c/o Iona Community, GIA Publications, Inc., agent.

11 10 11 4
JENNIFER

love   will   not   die.
you   still   will   stay.
we   hope   and   feel.
and   our   dear   child.

breathes with   your   breath.

This hymn may be read aloud while the following sequence is played.

66 There Is a Place

Unison

1 There is a place pre - pared for lit - tle chil - dren,
2 There is a place where hands which held ours tight - ly
3 There is a place where all the lost po - ten - tial
4 There is a place where God will hear our ques - tions,
5 Je - sus, who bids us be like lit - tle chil - dren,

those we once lived for, those we deep - ly mourn;
now are re - leased be - yond all hurt and fear,
yields its full prom - ise, finds its true in - tent;
suf - fer our an - ger, share our speech - less grief,
shields those our arms are yearn - ing to em - brace.

those who from play, from learn - ing and from laugh - ter
healed by that love which al - so feels our sor - row,
si - lenced no more, young voic - es ec - ho free - ly
gen - tly re - pair the in - no - cence of lov - ing
God will en - sure that all are re - u - nit - ed;

Text and music: John L. Bell, 1996.
© 1996 WGRG c/o Iona Community, GIA Publications, Inc., agent.

11 10 11 4
DUNBLANE PRIMARY

to Coda after v. 5

too   soon were   torn.
tear   af - ter   tear.
as   they were meant.
and   of be - lief.
there   is   a   place.

Coda

67 Be unto Your Name

Unison

1 We are a mo - ment, you are for - ev - er,
2 We are the bro - ken, you are the heal - er,

Lord of the a - ges, God be - fore time.
Je - sus, Re - deem - er, might - y to save.

We are a va - pour, you are e - ter - nal,
You are the love song we'll sing for - ev - er,

Love ev - er-last - ing, reign-ing on high.
bow - ing be-fore you, bless - ing your name.

Text and music: Lynn DeShazo and Gary Sadler, 1998.
© 1998 Integrity's Hosanna! Music (ASCAP).

10 9 10 9
BE UNTO YOUR NAME

68   Adoramus te, Domine Deus

Adoramus te, Domine Deus.
We adore you, O Lord God.

Text: Traditional
Music: Margaret Rizza, 1997. © 1997 Kevin Mayhew, Ltd.

Irregular
ADORAMUS TE

Heaven Is Singing/*El cielo canta alegría* 69

1 Heav - en is sing - ing for joy, al - le - lu - ia!
2 Heav - en is sing - ing for joy, al - le - lu - ia!
3 Heav - en is sing - ing for joy, al - le - lu - ia!
1 *El cie - lo can - ta a - le - grí - a, a - le - lu - ia!*
2 *El cie - lo can - ta a - le - grí - a, a - le - lu - ia!*
3 *El cie - lo can - ta a - le - grí - a, a - le - lu - ia!*

for in your life and in mine is shin - ing the
for your life and mine u - nite in the
for your life and mine will al - ways bear
por que en tu vi - da y la mí - a bri - lla la
por que en tu vi - da y la mí - a las une el
por que en tu vi - da y la mí - a pro - clam - ar -

glo - ry of God.
glo - ry of God.
wit - ness to God. Al - le - lu - ia!
glo - ria de Dios.
a - mor de Dios.
án al Señ - or.

Al - le - lu - ia! Al - le - lu - ia! Al - le - lu - ia!

Text and melody: Pablo Sosa, 1958. *Text and melody © GIA Publications, Inc.; arr. © WGRG c/o Iona Community, GIA Publications, Inc., agent.*

74 68 with refrain
ALEGRÍA

70 How Lovely Is Your Dwelling Place

1 How love-ly is your dwell-ing place, O Lord Al-might-
(2 One) thing I ask and I would seek: to see your beau-

y. For my soul longs and ev-en faints for
ty, to find you in the place your glo-ry

you. For here my heart is sat-is-fied,
dwells. One thing I ask and I would seek:

with-in your pres-ence. I sing be-neath the
to see your beau-ty, to find you in the

Text and music: Matt Redman, 1995; based on Psalm 84 and Psalm 27:4.
© 1995 Thankyou Music (PRS) admin. EMI CMG Publishing.

Irregular
BETTER IS ONE DAY

71 Grace Like Rain

1 A-maz - ing grace, how sweet the sound,
2 that taught my heart to fear,
3 we've been there ten thous - and years,

that saved a wretch like me. I once
and grace my fears re - lieved. How prec-
bright shin - ing as the sun, we've no

was lost but now I'm found, was blind
ious did that grace ap - pear the hour
less days to sing your praise than when

but now I see so clear - ly.
I first be - lieved.
we'd first be - gun.

Hal - le - lu - jah, grace like rain falls down

on me. Hal - le - lu - jah, all my stains

Fine (last time)

are washed a - way, they're washed a - way.

2 'Twas grace
3 When

Text: John Newton, 1779; refrain by Todd Agnew, 2003. *Refrain © 2003 Ardent/Koala Music.*   Irregular
Music: Todd Agnew, 2003. *© 2003 Ardent/Koala Music.*

Let My Spirit Always Sing

1 Let my spir-it al-ways sing, though my heart be
2 Though my bod-y be con-fined, let your word en-
3 Let your wis-dom grace my years, choose my words and
4 Let my spir-it al-ways sing, to your Spir-it

win-ter-ing, though the sea-son of de-spair
gage my mind. Let the in-ner eye dis-cern
chase my fears, give me wit to wel-come change,
an-swer-ing, through the si-lence, through the pain,

give no sign that you are there. God to whom my
how much more there is to learn, see the world be-
to ac-cept, and not es-trange. Let my joy be
know my hope is not in vain, like a feath-er

days be-long, let there al-ways be a song.
com-ing whole through the win-dow of the soul.
full and deep in the know-ledge that I keep.
on your breath trust your love, through life and death.

Text: Shirley Erena Murray, 1994. © 1996 Hope Publishing Co.
Music: Jane Marshall, 2005, ©, admin. Augsburg Fortress.

77 77 77
SPIRITSONG

73 *Nyanyikanlah/Hallelujah! Sing Praise*

Nya - nyi - kan - lah nya - nyi - an ba - ru ba - gi
1 Hal - le - lu - jah! Sing praise to your Cre - a - tor,
2 Praise the Lord, all moun - tains and o - ceans, roll - ing
3 Give to God all glo - ry and hon - our. From the

Tu - han, pen - cip - ta ca - kra - wa - la. Se -
sun, moon and stars and an - gels a - bove. Praise the
thun - der and wind and storm clouds on high. Praise the
depths to the heights let prais - es re - sound to the

ga - la se - ra - fim ke - ru - bim, pu - ji - lah
Lord, whose word es - tab - lished the heav - ens, who up -
Lord, your Mak - er, all liv - ing crea - tures, all the
Lord, the source of strength and sal - va - tion for all

Di - a be - sar - kan - lah Na - ma - Nya.
holds all the earth in pow - er and love.
beasts in the fields and birds in the sky.
peo - ple on whom God's fa - vour is found.

Text: Ps. 148, Indonesian para. Tilly Lubis, 2009. © *2009 Yamuger, Indonesian Institute*
for Sacred Music. English version. David Diephouse, 2009. © *2009 Faith Alive Christian Resources.*
Music: Melody Batak trad., Toba, Indonesia; arr. H.A. Pandopo, 2009, ©.

11 9 11 11 10 10

NYANYIKANLAH

Ber - so - rak so - rai ba - gi Ra - ja - mu!
God reigns on high, let the heav - ens re - joice! (Oh)
Both young and old, come and join in the song! (Oh)
Praise God, you saints who are claimed as God's own! (Oh)

Ber - so - rak so - rai ba - gi Ra - ja - mu!
God reigns on high, let the heav - ens re - joice!
Both young and old, come and join in the song!
Praise God, you saints who are claimed as God's own!

Holy, Holy, Holy/¡Santo, santo, santo! 74

Ho - ly, ho - ly, ho - ly, my heart, my heart a - dores you! My
¡San - to, san - to, san - to, mi co - ra - zón te a - do - ra! Mi

heart is glad to say the words: you are ho - ly, Lord.
co - ra - zón te sa - be de - cir: san - to e - res Se - ñor.

Text: Argentine trad.
Music: Melody Argentine trad.; arr. Wild Goose Worship Group, Iona Community.
Arr. © 1990 WGRG c/o Iona Community, GIA Publications, Inc., agent.

67 85
ARGENTINE SANTO

75 Hallelujah, Hallelujah, Praise the Name

1 The name of God be for-ev-er blest by ev-ery
2 God is ex-alt-ed; he reigns on high, but looks be-

na-tion from east to west. Come now and glad-ly
low with a lov-ing eye to raise the need-y

his name con-fess: there is no one like
and poor who cry. There is no one like

[1,3] our God. [2,4] our God! Hal-le

Text: Ps.113, para. Boulos Boshra, 2002. © 2002 Songs of the Evangelical Presbyterian
    Church of Egypt; admin. Faith Alive Christian Resources. Tr. Anne Emile Zaki, 2009.
    © 2009 Faith Alive Christian Resources. Vers. Emily Brink, 2009. © 2009 Faith Alive Christian Resources.
Music: Boulos Boshra, 2002. © 2002 Songs of the Evangelical Presbyterian Church of Egypt;
    admin. Faith Alive Christian Resources.

99 98 with refrain

76 Hear My Cry, O God, and Save Me

1 Hear my cry, O God, and save me! Trou - bles
2 You, O God, once walked be - side me. In the
3 All cre - a - tion bows be - fore you; saints in

and dis - tress en - slave me. Day and night I seek your face,
night your songs re - vived me. Were your prom - is - es in vain?
earth and heaven a - dore you. Thun - der roars and tor - rents fall

yearn - ing for your light and grace. But these eyes, they
Will you smile on me a - gain? Long a - go you
at your word, O God of all! In our grief, you

Text: Ps. 77, para. Michael Morgan, 2011, ©, admin. *Faith Alive Christian Resources.*
Music: *Genevan Psalter*, 1551; harm. Claude Goudimel, 1564.

88 77D
GENEVAN 77

can - not see you; out - stretched arms, they can - not feel you.
brought re - demp - tion; your right hand won our sal - va - tion.
stand be - side us, there to lift us and to guide us,

My heart breaks in deep de - spair;
I re - mem - ber deeds of old:
un - seen Sav - iour of our days,

my soul longs to hold you here.
now, re - mem - ber me, O Lord!
heir to end - less songs of praise!

77 My Soul Cries Out

1 My soul cries out with a joy - ful shout that the
2 Though I am small, my God, my all, you
3 From the halls of power to the for - tress tower not a
4 Though the na - tions rage from age to age we re -

God of my heart is great, and my spir - it sings of the
work great things in me, and your mer - cy will last from the
stone will be left on stone. Let the king be - ware, for your
mem - ber who holds us fast: God's mer - cy must de -

won - drous things that you bring to the ones who wait. You
depths of the past to the end of the age to be. Your
jus - tice tears ev - ery ty - rant from his throne. The
liv - er us from the con - quer-or's crush - ing grasp. This

fixed your sight on your ser - vant's plight, and my
ver - y name puts the proud to shame, and to
hun - gry poor shall weep no more for the
sav - ing word that our fore - bears heard is the

Text: Rory Cooney, based on Luke 1.46–58.
Music: Melody Irish trad.; arr. Rory Cooney.
Text and arr. © 1990 GIA Publications, Inc.

Irregular
STAR OF THE COUNTY DOWN

78 O God of Matchless Glory

1 O God of match-less glo - ry, of all sur-
2 With Wis - dom as your part - ner you formed the
3 Your word gives life for - ev - er; our fear of

pass - ing worth, you fill the world with
earth and sea; and still she calls the
death is stilled. With liv - ing bread and

won - der, you bring the stars to birth. To
sim - ple, "Be wise and learn from me." Who
wa - ter our deep - est need is filled. To

Text: Ruth Duck, 1989. © 1992 GIA Publications, Inc.
Music: Ruth Watson Henderson, 1995, ©.

76 76 76 89
HASTINGS

79 Out of the Depths of Fear

1 Out of the depths of fear we cry to you, O
2 Out of the depths of grief we cry to you, O
3 Out of the depths of faith we cry to you, O

God. The world we know is shak - en;
God. Our hearts are cracked and bro - ken;
God. Though light's al - most ex - tin - guished

our cer - tain-ties are lost. Heart-wear - y and for -
we're hol - low with this loss. Your prom-is - es seem
and trust is lost in fear, we turn to you in

Text: Ellen Clark-King, 2014.
Music: Lim Swee Hong, 2014. *Text and music © 2014 Hope Publishing Co.*

66 76 76 8
DI MANA ALLAH

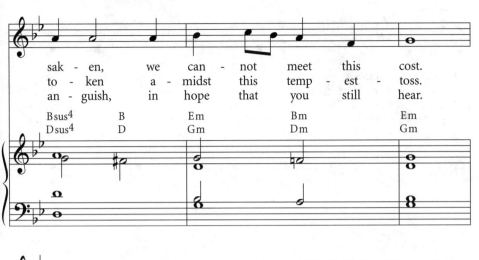

sak - en,   we   can - not   meet   this   cost.
to - ken   a - midst   this   temp - est - toss.
an - guish,   in   hope   that   you   still   hear.

Bsus⁴   B   Em   Bm   Em
Dsus⁴   D   Gm   Dm   Gm

We   are   a - fraid—   where   are   you,   God?
We   are   in   grief—   where   are   you,   God?
We   are   your   own—   where   are   you,   God?

Am⁷   Em/G   CM⁷   Bsus⁴   B
Cm⁷   Gm/B♭   E♭M⁷   Dsus⁴   D

80 O God, Why Are You Silent?

1 O God, why are you si - lent? I
2 Now lost with - in my griev - ing, I
3 My hope lies bruised and bat - tered, my
4 Through end - less nights of weep - ing, through
5 May pain draw forth com - pas - sion, let

can - not hear your voice. The proud and strong and
fall and lose my way, my frag - ile, faint be -
wound - ed heart is torn; my spir - it spent and
wear - y days of grief, my heart is in your
wis - dom rise from loss. O take my heart and

vio - lent all claim you and re - joice. You
liev - ing so swift - ly swept a - way. O
shat - tered by life's re - lent - less storm. Will
keep - ing, my com - fort, my re - lief. Come,
fash - ion the im - age of your cross. Then

Text: Marty Haugen, 2003. © 2003 GIA Publications, Inc.
Music: Hans Leo Hassler, 1601; arr. J.S. Bach, 1729.

76 76D
PASSION CHORALE

prom-ised you would hold   me with ten - der - ness and   care. Draw
God   of   pain and   sor - row, my com-pass and my   guide,   I
you   not bend to   hear   me, my   cries from deep with - in?   Have
share my tears and   sad - ness; come, suf - fer   in   my   pain;   O
may   I   know your heal - ing through heal-ing that   I   share, your

near,   O   Love, en - fold   me, and   ease the pain   I   bear.
can - not face the   mor - row with - out   you   by   my   side.
you   no   word to   cheer   me when night   is   clos - ing   in?
bring me home to   glad - ness, re - store my hope   a - gain.
grace and love re - veal - ing your ten - der - ness and   care.

81 O Beauty Ever Ancient

1 O beau-ty ev - er an - cient, O beau-ty ev - er new,
2 O beau-ty in cre - a - tion, in world of sound and sight,
3 O beau-ty that is move - ment in li - quid line of grace,
4 O beau-ty of the Spir - it where love is shin - ing through,

di - vine and Ho - ly Pres - ence, my be - ing sings to you,
O beau - ty in the si - lence, in dark-ness as in light,
O beau - ty that is still - ness in love - ly form or face,
O beau - ty ev - er an - cient, O beau - ty ev - er new,

in gra - ti-tude, in wor - ship my be - ing sings to you!
in gra - ti-tude, in wor - ship my be - ing sings to you!
in gra - ti-tude, in wor - ship my be - ing sings to you!
in gra - ti-tude, in wor - ship my be - ing sings to you!

Text: Shirley Erena Murray, 2000. © 2000 Hope Publishing Co.
Music: Alfred V. Fedak, 2007. © 2009 Selah Publishing Co.

76 76 76
ANCIENT BEAUTY

Praise, Praise, Praise the Lord! 82

Praise, praise, praise the Lord! Praise God's ho - ly name. Al - le - lu - ia!
Lou - ez le Sei - gneur! Lou - ez son saint nom. Al - le - lu - ia!

Praise, praise, praise the Lord! Praise God's ho - ly name. Al - le - lu - ia!
Lou - ez le Sei - gneur! Lou - ez son saint nom. Al - le - lu - ia!

Praise God's ho - ly name. Al - le - lu - ia!
Lou - ez son saint nom. Al - le - lu - ia!

Praise God's ho - ly name. Al - le - lu - ia!
Lou - ez son saint nom. Al - le - lu - ia!

Praise God's ho - ly name. Al - le - lu - ia!
Lou - ez son saint nom. Al - le - lu - ia!

Praise God's ho - ly name. Al - le - lu - ia!
Lou - ez son saint nom. Al - le - lu - ia!

This song may be repeated, adding a vocal part on each repetition:
melody (alto) alone; melody + tenor; melody + lower parts; all voices.

Text: Cameroon trad.
Music: Cameroon processional, arr. Ralph M. Johnson, 1994. © *1994 earthsongs.*

Irregular
CAMEROON PRAISE

83 Though Hope Desert My Heart

1 Though hope de - sert my heart,
2 Though con - fi - dence run dry,
3 There is no threat - ening place,
4 In Christ who, on the cross,
5 I will not dread the dark,

though
though
no
felt
the

strange - ness fill my soul,
wear - y flesh be sore,
tri - al I could know
all our hurt and more,
fate be - yond con - trol,

though truth tor - ment my
though con - ver - sa - tion
which has not known your
and cried in deep a -
nor fear what reigns in

trou - bled mind, you have been here be - fore.
bear no fruit, you have been here be - fore.
pres - ence first: you have been here be - fore.
ban - don - ment, you have been here be - fore.
fright - ening things: you will be there be - fore.

Text and music: John L. Bell, 2005.
© 2005 WGRG c/o Iona Community, GIA Publications, Inc., agent.

SM
CALABRIA

Praise God for This Holy Ground

Unison

1 Praise God for this ho - ly ground,
2 Praise God in whose word we find
3 Praise God who through Christ makes known
4 Praise God's Spir - it who be - friends,
5 Though praise ends, praise is be - gun

place and peo - ple, sight and sound.
food for bod - y, soul, and mind.
all are loved and called God's own.
rais - es, hum - bles, breaks, and mends.
where God's will is glad - ly done.

Hal - le - lu - jah! Hal - le - lu - jah! Hal - le - lu - jah! God's

Last Time

good - ness is e - ter - nal.

Text and music: John L. Bell, 2002.

77 12 7
HEYMONYSTRAAT

85 God of the Bible

1 God of the Bible, God in the Gospel,
2 God in our struggles, God in our hunger,
3 Those without status, those who are nothing,
4 Not by your finger, not by your anger
5 Hope we must carry, shining and certain,

hope seen in Jesus, hope yet to come,
suffering with us, taking our part,
you have made royal, gifted with rights,
will our world order change in a day,
through all our turmoil, terror and loss,

you are our centre, daylight or darkness,
still you empow'r us, mothering Spirit,
chosen as partners, midwives of justice,
but by your people, fearless and faithful,
bonding us gladly, one to the other,

Text: Shirley Erena Murray, 1995. © 1996 Hope Publishing Co.
Music: Tony E. Alonso, 2001. © 2001 GIA Publications, Inc.

55 54D with refrain
GOD OF THE BIBLE

free - dom or pris - on, you are our home.
feed - ing, sus - tain - ing from your own heart.
birth - ing new sys - tems, light - ing new lights.
small pa - per lan - terns light - ing the way.
till our world chang - es, fac - ing the Cross.

Refrain

Fresh as the morn - ing, sure as the sun - rise, God al - ways faith - ful, you do not change. Fresh as the morn - ing, sure as the sun - rise, God al - ways faith - ful, you do not change.

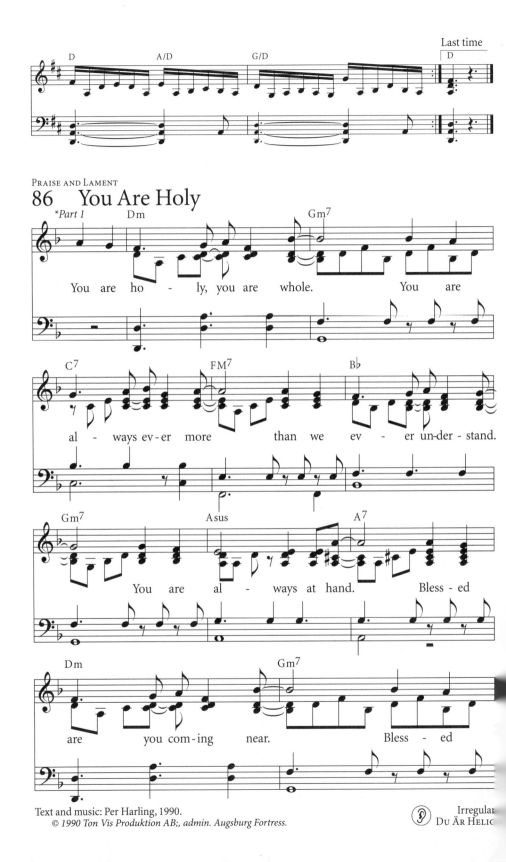

PRAISE AND LAMENT

86 You Are Holy

Part 1

You are ho - ly, you are whole. You are al - ways ev - er more than we ev - er un-der - stand. You are al - ways at hand. Bless - ed are you com - ing near. Bless - ed

Text and music: Per Harling, 1990.
© 1990 Ton Vis Produktion AB;, admin. Augsburg Fortress.

Irregular
Du Är Helig

in the high - est! Sing ho -

san - na! Sing ho - san - na to our God!

87 Give Thanks to the Lord Our God

Give thanks   to the Lord our   God,   for our God is
Ren - dei   gra - ças ao Sen - hor,   por - que e - le é

good,   ver - y   good;   for God's   lov - ing -
bom,   e - le é   bom;   por que   su - a mise - ri -

Text: Ps. 106, v.1 and 48, para. Fiona Vidal-White, 2005, ©.
Music: Melody Brazil; arr. Michael Capon, 2016.
Music © World Council of Churches; arr. Michael Capon, © 2016.

Irregular

88 Give Thanks for Life

Unison

1 Give thanks for life, the meas - ure of our days;
2 Give thanks for those who made their life a light
3 And for our own, our liv - ing and our dead,
4 Give thanks for hope, that like the wheat, the grain

mor - tal we pass through beau - ty that de - cays, yet
caught from the Christ - flame, burst - ing through the night, who
thanks for the love by which our life is fed, a
ly - ing in dark - ness, does its life re - tain in

sing to God our hope, our love, our praise:
touched the truth, who burned for what is right:
love not changed by time or death or dread:
re - sur - rec - tion to grow green a - gain:

hal - le - lu - jah, hal - le - lu - jah!

Text: Shirley Erena Murray, 1987. © 1987 Hope Publishing Co.
Music: Ralph Vaughan Williams, 1906. © Oxford University Press.

10 10 10 with Alleluias
SINE NOMINE

Triangle and/or finger cymbals

1. Praise to God, praise to God for the green-ness
2. Thanks to God, thanks to God for the gift of
3. Glo - ry to God, glo - ry to God for the grace of

of the trees, for the beau - ty of the flow'rs,
friends in Christ, for the church, our house of faith,
Christ, the Son, for the love of par - ent God,

for the blue-ness of the sky, for the great-ness of the sea.
for the gift of won-drous love, for the gift of end-less grace.
for the com-fort and the strength of the Spir - it, ho - ly God.

Praise to God, praise to God now and for - ev - er - more.
Thanks to God, thanks to God now and for - ev - er - more.
Glo - ry to God, glo - ry to God now and for - ev - er - more.

Text: Nobuaki Hanaoka, 1980, alt., © Abingdon Press, admin. Music Services.
Music: Japan trad.

Irregular
SAKURA

90 *Shukuru Yesu*/Thanking You, Jesus

Swahili   Asanti, Asanti, Yesu.
Bari (Sudanese dialect)   Tinati, Tinati, Yesu.
Luganda   Webale, Webale, Yesu.

Text: Sudanese worship chorus. *Text © 2007 East Africa Annual Conference, admin. General Board of Global Ministries t/a GBG Musik.*
Music: Arr. Greg Scheer, 2007. *Music Arr. © 2007 Greg Scheer, admin. General Board of Global Ministries t/a GBG Musik.*

Irregular
SHUKURU YESU

We Give Our Thanks/*Reamo leboga* 91

F   C   Dm

1 *Re - a - mo le - bo - ga, re - a - mo*
2 We give our thanks to God, we give our
3 *Nous ren - dons grâce à Dieu, nous ren - dons*

Gm   F   C

le - bo - ga, re - a - mo
thanks to God, we give our
grâce à Dieu, nous ren - dons

F   C   Dm   Bb   F/C   C7   F

le - bo - ga mo - di - mo wa ro - na.
thanks to God, we give our thanks to God.
grâce à Dieu, nous ren - dons grâce à Dieu.

Optional English Verses:

We give our hands to you, (3x)
because you reached for us.

We give our eyes to you, (3x)
because your looked for us.

We give our feet to you, (3x)
because you walk with us.

We give our hearts to you, (3x)
because you first loved us.

Tswana pronounciation: Ray-yoh-moh lay-boh-gah
(the "g" in "gah" should be closer to an aspirated "h" than a "g").

Text and music: Botswana trad., as taught by Daisy Nshakazongwe. English para. and transcr.:   66 66
I-to Loh. French tr.: David Fines, 2006. Additional English verses: Andrew Donaldson. REAMO LEBOGA
English para. and transcr. © 1986 World Council of Churches and the Asian Institute for Liturgy and Music.
French tr. © 2006 David Fines. Additional English verses © Andrew Donaldson.

92 In Sacred Manner May We Walk

1 In sa-cred man-ner may we walk up-on the fair and lov-ing
2 In sa-cred man-ner may we see the lu-mi-nous and lov-ing
3 In sa-cred man-ner may we touch the sus-pi-rant and lov-ing
4 In sa-cred man-ner may we hear the pound-ing waves, the scar-ing

earth, in beau-ty move, in beau-ty love the
stars, with won-der and with awe be-hold their
green. Give hon-our and give grat-i-tude for
fire, the rush-ing wind, the sing-ing night, the

liv-ing round that brought us birth. We stand on ho-ly
ev-er new cre-a-tive pow'rs. The heav-ens show us
shade, for bloom, for gift un-seen. The trees shall shout for
for-est hymn, the lov-ing choir. The morn-ing stars shall

Text: Susan Palo Cherwien, 1997, ©; admin. Augsburg Fortress.
Music: Thomas Pavlechko, 2008. © Augsburg Fortress.

88 88 86
TEAGUE

ground.   We stand on ho - ly ground.
God.   The heav - ens show us God.
joy.   The trees shall shout for joy.
sing.   The morn - ing stars shall sing.

joy, shout for joy,
sing, shall sing.

5 In sacred manner may we live
  among the wise and loving ones,
  sit humbly, as at sages' feet,
  by four-legged, finned, and feathered ones.
  The animals will teach.

6 In sacred manner may we walk
  upon the fair and loving earth,
  in beauty move, in beauty love
  the living round that brought us birth.
  We stand on holy ground.

93 Lord, Your Hands Have Formed This World

1 Lord, your hands have formed this world, ev-ery part is
2 Yours the soil that holds the seed, you give warmth and
3 Like a mat you roll out land— space to build, for
1 I - meg - moy pi - tak ay yay I - meg - moh a-

shaped by you— wa-ter rum - bling o - ver rocks, air and
mois - ture too— sprout-ing bloss - oms, crops and buds, trees and
us and you, earth - ly homes and, bet - ter still, homes for
da - tak - lay, I - meg - moh a - da - da - nom, Eg - gew

sun - light: each day's signs that you make all things new.
plants: the sea - son's signs that you make all things new.
Christ: the tru - est sign that you make all things new.
tan wa - day e - dom, Ga - yom ni hi - ga - mi.

Text: Ramon and Salio Oliano; Eng. version James Minchin and Delbert Rice.
Eng. version © James Minchin, Asian Institute for Liturgy and Music.
Music: Melody Ikalahan trad. (Philippines); arr. John L. Bell, 1991.
Music arr. © 1991 WGRG c/o Iona Community, GIA Publications, Inc., agent.

77 776
GAYOM NI HIGAMI

From the Highest of Heights

1 From the high-est of heights to the depths of the sea,
2 Who has told ev-ery lighten - ing bolt where it should go,

cre - a - tion's re - veal - ing your maj - es -
or seen heaven-ly store-house-es la - den with

ty. From the col-ours of fall to the fra-grance of
snow? Who i-mag-ined the sun and gives source to its

Text: Laura Story and Jesse Reeves, 2002.
Music: Laura Story, 2002. *Text and music © 2004 worshiptogether.com Songs (ASCAP)/
sixsteps Music (ASCAP)/Gleaning Publishing (ASCAP); admin. EMI CMG Publishing.*

Irregular
INDESCRIBABLE

95 We're Bound on a Journey

1 We're bound on a jour-ney a-cross the wide wa-ters; we
2 Our sail-ing com-pan-ions are all liv-ing spe-cies— we'd
3 God gave us a gar-den so care-ful-ly plant-ed its

sail in the dark to a har-bour un-known. The
have to make room if the di-no-saurs came— and
fruits should sus-tain us for ev-er and aye; Oh!

birds and the beasts and all God's sons and daugh-ters, our
nei-ther for them nor for us is it ea-sy to-
nev-er a-gain will we take it for grant-ed or

ship is a plan-et and we are a-lone. Take
ge-ther so cramped in this shake-a-ble frame. Take
need-less-ly gam-ble our birth-right a-way! Take

Text: Elliot Rose. © *Estate of Elliot Rose.*
Music: Melody Becca Whitla, 1994, ©; harm. Michael Capon, 2014, ©.

12 11 12 11D
JOURNEY

heart and good cheer though the floods are a - ris - ing; we
heart and good cheer you poor pan - ther and bi - son, poor
heart and good cheer while the floods are a - ris - ing; we'll

hear the rain fall and we hear the storm roar, but be -
wood - louse, and shrew mouse, tho' tri - als be sore. Our
join heart and hand on Mount Ar - a - rat's shore. This

yond are the hands that the whole world re - lies on: our
Cap - tain we have to the fur - thest ho - ri - zon, our
world is for cher - ish - ing, lov - ing and prais - ing our

Mak - er, Re - deem - er and friend ev - er - more.

96 All Creation Danced in Answer

1 All creation danced in answer when God's
2 Jesus gave the tune new texture, love song
3 And the Spirit comes, composing music
4 Come, my friends, sing, dance in answer as God's

voice first touched the air and the great eternal
for a world set free: gospel sung in full, rich
made of wind and fire, in its new-found tones dis-
music fills the air and the great eternal

cantor called a universe to prayer, called to
measure, earth's voice, but God's melody; passion
closing all the heart and soul require, forging
cantor calls us yet to praise and prayer, bids us

Text: John Core, 2006. © 2006 Wayne Leupold Editions, Inc.
Music: Patrick Michaels, 2014, ©.

87 87D
ETERNAL CANTOR

praise and to thanks - giv - ing all that filled the space a -
mu - sic, sad and som - bre, dis - cord on a cross was
from day's hum and thun - der, from that mix - ture sweet and
join the end - less sing - ing, till all earth - ly song shall

bout, sought a hymn from all things
built, giv - ing way to bright new
strong, psalms and hymns of awe and
cease; heav - en's voice a - lone goes

liv - ing, bid the stones them - selves cry out.
tim - bre in the Eas - ter morn - ing's lilt.
won - der: dai - ly life as sa - cred song.
ring - ing through a u - ni - verse at peace.

97 God Is Calling through the Whisper

1 God is call - ing through the whis - per of the Spir - it's deep-est
2 God is call - ing through the voic - es of our neigh-bours' ur - gent
3 God is call - ing through the mu - sic of sub - lime and hu - man

sighs, through the thrill of sud - den beau - ties that can
prayers, through their long - ing for re - demp - tion and for
arts, through the hymns of earth and an - gels, and the

catch us by sur - prise. Flash of light - ning, crash of
res - cue from de - spair. Place of hurt or face or
car - ols of our hearts. Lift of joy and gift of

thun - der; hush of still - ness, rush of won - der: God is
need - ing; stri - dent cry or si - lent plead - ing: God is
sing - ing; days and nights our prais-es bring - ing: God is

Text: Mary Louise Bringle, 2003. © 2006 GIA Publications, Inc.
Music: Melody Polish trad., harm. Philip M. Young, 2005, ©, alt.

87 87 88 77
W ZLOBIE LEZY

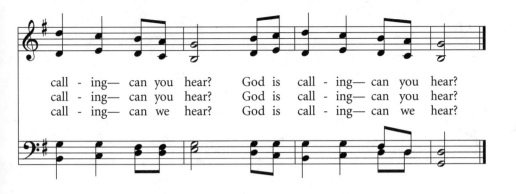

call - ing— can you hear? God is call - ing— can you hear?
call - ing— can you hear? God is call - ing— can you hear?
call - ing— can we hear? God is call - ing— can we hear?

Take, O Take Me/*Oh! Prends-moi tel que je suis* 98

Take, O take me as I am; sum - mon out what I shall
Oh! Prends - moi tel que je suis; fais - moi vi - vre que pour

be; set your seal up - on my heart and live in me.
toi. Viens, mets ton sceau sur mon cœur; viens vi - vre en moi.

Text: John L. Bell, 1995. French tr. David Fines, 2005. *French trans.* © 2005 David Fines. 77 74
Music: John L. Bell, 1995. *Text and music:*
   © 1995 WGRG c/o Iona Community, GIA Publications, Inc., agent.

99 Listen Up!

1 In the si - lence of peace - ful nights,
2 In the ques - tions of fu - ture paths,
3 In the qui - et where thoughts run free

in the cha - os of stress - ful lives,
in re - flec - tions of days gone past,
in the gath' - ring of two or three

in the prom - ise of wa - ter poured,
in the hear - ing of Word pro - claimed,
in the giv - ing of wine and bread

God calls— lis - ten, can you hear it?

God calls— whis - pers of the Spir - it.

Chorus

Lis-ten up! Lis-ten up! God is call - ing. Lis-ten up! Lis-ten up!

God is call - ing for you. Lis - ten up! Lis - ten up!

3rd time to Coda

God is call - ing. Lis - ten now.

Text: Dennis Hendricksen and Sara Wahl, 2004.
Music: Sarah Sedgman and Sara Wahl, 2004.
Text and music © 2004 Evangelical Lutheran Church in Canada.

Irregular
LISTEN UP

100 Listen, God Is Calling/*Neno lake Mungu*

Refrain

Leader / **All**

Lis - ten, lis - ten, God is call - ing, through the Word in - vit - ing,
Ne - no, ne - no la - ke Mu - ngu la - ku - i - ta we - we,

of - fer - ing for - give - ness, com - fort, and joy. [1 *Leader*] Lis - ten. [2] joy.
ne - no la wo - ko - vu, te na je - ma. ma.

Leader / **All**

1 Je - sus gave his man - date: share the good news
2 Let none be for - got - ten through - out the world.
3 Help us to be faith - ful, stand - ing stead - fast,
1 *Ye - su a - li - se - ma, Mka - hu - bi - ri.*

Leader / **All** / **Leader** (*to Refrain*)

that he came to save us and set us free. Lis - ten.
In the tri - une name of God, go and bap - tize.
walk - ing in your pre - cepts, led by your Word.
Ne - no la - ke Mu - ngu la wo - ko - vu.

Text: Tanzanian trad.; trans. Howard S. Olson, 1968.
Trans. © Makumira University College, admin. Augsburg Fortress.
Music: Tanzanian trad.; arr. C. Michael Hawn, 2001, ©.

64 64 *with refrain*
NENO LAKE MUNGU

If You Love Me 101

1 If you love me, tru - ly love me, keep my com - mand - ments
2 If you love me, tru - ly love me, come now and my dis -
4 If you love me, tru - ly love me, in - to the world a -

day by day. If you love me, tru - ly love me,
ci - ple be. If you love me, tru - ly love me,
rise and go. If you love me, tru - ly love me,

fol - low for - ev - er in my way.
fol - low and so re - mem - ber me.
there ev - ery - where my wit - ness show.

to verse three

3 Through the land my peo - ple feed, al - le - lu - ia,

in their sor - row, in their need, al - le - lu - ia.

Text and music: Natalie Sleeth, 1980. © *1980 Hinshaw Music, Inc.*

Irregular
IF YOU LOVE ME

102 Somebody's Knocking at Your Door

Some-bod-y's knock-in' at your door; some-bod-y's

knock-in' at your door; O sin-ner, why don't you

an-swer? Some-bod-y's knock-in' at your door.

1 Knocks like Je - sus,
2 Can't you hear him?
3 Je - sus calls you,   Some - bod - y's knock-in' at your door.
4 Can't you trust him?

Text and music: African-American spiritual; harm. Richard Proulx, 1986.
Harm. © 1986 GIA Publications, Inc.

Irregular
SOMEBODY'S KNOCKING

Knocks like Je - sus,
Can't you hear him?
Je - sus calls you, Some - bod - y's knock-in' at your door.
Can't you trust him?

O sin - ner, why don't you an - swer?

Some - bod - y's knock - in' at your door.

103 The Call Is Clear and Simple

1 The call is clear and sim - ple: "Love God and hu - man -
2 God, help us sort our mo - tives, that lov - ing may be
3 God, teach us strength and wis - dom when false love takes the
4 O wise and ho - ly Lov - er, teach us, as sea - sons

kind;" but love de - mands much wis - dom and
whole. High aims or base am - bi - tion? Com -
lead. Too well we learn sub - mis - sion and
turn, to know our - selves and oth - ers— deep,

clar - i - ty of mind. "Be wi - ly as a
pas - sion or con - trol? Then help us clear our
si - lence our own need. When oth - ers would mis -
hon - est love to learn. So may we nur - ture

Text: Ruth Duck, 1992. © 1992 GIA Publications, Inc.
Music: Finnish trad.; harm. David Evans. *Harm.* © Oxford University Press.

76 76D
NYLAND

ser - pent, though gen - tle as a dove," for
sched - ules of ev - ery fran - tic task that
use us or lure us toward the wrong, God,
liv - ing in all we say and do, in

man - y are the dan - gers up - on the path of love.
leads a - way from do - ing the one thing that you ask.
tem - per love with cour - age to keep our bound-aries strong.
strong and gen - tle giv - ing to hu - man - kind and you.

104 Love the Lord Your God

Love the Lord your God with all your heart. Love the Lord your God with all your soul.

Capo 4

Text and music: Jean and Jim Strathdee, 1991. © 1991 Desert Flower Music.

Irregular
GREAT COMMANDMENT

all   that   you   are.

When Jesus Saw the Fishermen 105

1 When Je - sus saw the fish - er - men in
2 They fol - lowed where he healed the sick and
3 And now his friends are ev - ery - where; the

boats up - on the sea, he called to them, "Come,
gave the hun - gry bread, and oth - ers joined them
cir - cle once so small ex - tends a - round the

leave your nets and fol - low, fol - low me."
as they went, wher - ev - er Je - sus led.
whole wide world, for Je - sus calls us all.

May be sung as a round.

Text: Edith Agnew, 1953. © 1953 W. L. Jenkins; admin. Westminster John Knox Press.
Music: Richard L. Van Oss, 1992. © 1994 Faith Alive Publications.

CM
ST STEPHEN

106 Come to Me, O Weary Traveller

1 Come to me, O wear-y trav-eller; come to me with your dis-tress; come to me, you heav-y-bur-dened; come to me and find your rest.

2 Do not fear, my yoke is eas-y; do not fear, my bur-den's light; do not fear the path be-fore you; do not run from me in fright.

3 Take my yoke and leave your trou-bles; take my yoke and come with me. Take my yoke, I am be-side you; take and learn hu-mil-i-ty.

4 Rest in me, O wear-y trav-eller; rest in me and do not fear. Rest in me, my heart is gen-tle; rest and cast a-way your care.

Text: Sylvia Dunstan, 1991. © 1991 GIA Publications, Inc.
Music: William P. Rowan, 1992. © 1993 Selah Publishing Co.

I Long for Your Commandments 107

1 I long for your com-mand-ments; your judg-ments all are good.
2 With-out your lamp to guide me I wan-der from the way.
3 Oh, how I love your know-ledge, more prec-ious than pure gold.

With-in your word is wis-dom; your teach-ings un-der-stood
With-out your laws and pre-cepts I stum-ble in the dark.
It sat-is-fies like hon-ey, a sweet-ness on my tongue.

are com-fort to my spir-it's need and in the night my
Your un-der-stand-ings are my hope that I may run in
It leads me to sal-va-tion's door where you have spread your

so - lace. Your stat - utes are my song.
free - dom. Your ways are my re - lease.
ta - ble. O, lead me to your home.

Text: Jean Janzen, 1991, ©.
Music: Heinrich Schütz, 1628.

76 76 876
WOHL DENEN, DIE DA WANDELN

108 How Glad I Was to Hear the News

1 How glad I was to hear the news: we're
2 We have no guide who knows the ground, but
3 We heard the wind blow all the night up -
4 Now all the land is waste and wild that
5 Proud is the town of Jer - i - cho and

free of Phar - oah's hand! It's pack on back and
signs by night and day. The fi - re knows where
on the wa - ters wide. As they stood high to
we just jour - ney through. But bread for wom - an,
cir - cled by a wall. Now hark - en how the

take the road un - to the Prom - ised Land. And it's
we are bound; the cloud will show the way. And it's
left and right we made the oth - er side. And it's
man, and child fall with the morn - ing dew. And it's
trum - pets blow and down the tow - ers fall. And it's

Text: Elliot Rose, ©.
Music: Melody English trad.; arr. Michael Capon, 2017, ©.

86 86 86 66
BLOW AWAY THE MORNING DEW

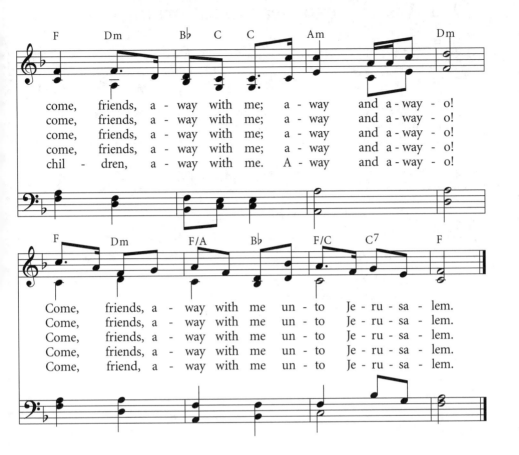

come, friends, a - way with me; a - way and a - way - o!
come, friends, a - way with me; a - way and a - way - o!
come, friends, a - way with me; a - way and a - way - o!
come, friends, a - way with me; a - way and a - way - o!
chil - dren, a - way with me. A - way and a - way - o!

Come, friends, a - way with me un - to Je - ru - sa - lem.
Come, friends, a - way with me un - to Je - ru - sa - lem.
Come, friends, a - way with me un - to Je - ru - sa - lem.
Come, friends, a - way with me un - to Je - ru - sa - lem.
Come, friend, a - way with me un - to Je - ru - sa - lem.

109 I Was There to Hear Your Borning Cry

1,4 "I was there to hear your born - ing cry; I'll be
2 "When you heard the won - der of the Word, I was
3 "In the mid - dle a - ges of your life, not too

there when you are old. I re - joiced the day you
there to cheer you on. You were raised to praise the
old, no long - er young, I'll be there to guide you

were bap - tized to see your life un - fold.
liv - ing Lord to whom you now be - long.
through the night, com - plete what I've be - gun.

Text and music: John Ylvisaker, 1985, ©.

97 96D
WATERLIFE

C   G

I was there when you were but a child   with a
If you find some - one to share your time   and you
When the eve - ning gen - tly clos - es in   and you

Am   D   G   C

faith to suit you well; in a blaze of light you
join your hearts as one, I'll be there to make your
shut your wear - y eyes, I'll be there as I have

For st. 4, D.C. st. 1 *al fine*

Bm⁷   Em   A⁷   D

wan - dered off to find where de - mons dwell."
vers - es rhyme from dusk till ris - ing sun."
al - ways been with just one more sur - prise."

110 I Will Not Abandon You

1 When the pain's too deep to sail and a-ny
2 (When your) dreams seem set a-side, no burn-ing
3 (No depth too) great, no width too wide, no night too

strength you had has failed, when no ho-ri-zon
bush, no tongues of fire, when you doubt I'll
dark no height too high that my love will

is in view, I will not a-ban-don you.
lead you through, I will not a-ban-don you.
not pur-sue; I will not a-ban-don you.

Fine

Text and music: Jaylene Johnson, 2014, ©; arr. Michael Capon, 2018, ©.

Irregular

Wait and rest, watch and pray, trust and hope; don't lose faith.

2 When your
3 No depth too

111 In a Deep, Unbounded Darkness

1 In a deep, un - bound - ed dark - ness
2 Though our world is ev - er - chang - ing,
3 Joy trans - forms our lips to boast - ing
4 God of Hag - ar, God of Sar - ah,

long be - fore the first light shone,
you are cons - tant, firm, and sure,
on - ly in your match - less grace,
God of no - mad A - bra - ham,

you, O God, bey - ond all mer - it,
faith - ful to your cov - enant prom - ise.
send - ing Christ to dwell a - mong us,
God of Mir - iam, God of Mos - es,

worked a won - der faith makes known:
Trust - ing you, we live se - cure,
Word made flesh in time and space:
Fier - y Pil - lar, great I AM:

in your mer - cy, in your mer - cy,
sing - ing prais - es, sing - ing prais - es
Friend and Sav - iour, Friend and Sav - iour,
lead us home - ward, lead us home - ward

you em - braced us as your own
long as heart and breath en - dure,
in whose life we glimpse your face
to the love - feast of the Lamb

ev - er - more and ev - er - more.
ev - er - more and ev - er - more.
ev - er - more and ev - er - more.
ev - er - more and ev - er - more.

Text: Anon. Chinese; trans. Francis P. Jones, 1953; adapt. Mary Louise Bringle, 2012.
Text © 2012 GIA Publications, Inc.
Music: Melody plainsong, Mode 8 (12th cent.?); adapt. *Piae Cantiones*, 1582.

87 87 87 7
DIVINUM MYSTERIUM

If You Only Have Faith/*Si tuvieras fe*   112

Text: Caribbean Pentecostal chorus; English tr. Pablo Sosa, 2006, alt.
English tr. © 2006 GIA Publications, Inc.
Music: Caribbean Pentecostal chorus; transcr. and harm. Jorge Lockward, 2008.
Music transcr. and harm. © 2008 General Board of Global Ministries t/a GBGMusik.

Irregular
SI TUVIERAS FE

move a - way, will move a - way, will move a -
mo - ve - rá, *se mo - ve - rá,* *se mo - ve -*

B7
D7

Repeat ad lib | *Last time*

way. And then the moun - tain will move a - way.
rá. *Y la mon - ta - ña se mo - ve - rá.*

Em
Gm

Em
Gm

113 Kneeling in the Dust to Form Us

1 Kneel-ing in the dust to form us, mould-ing with a pot-ter's care,
2 Shaped of flesh and bone and sin-ew, sound-ing cham-bers for the Word,
3 Tem-pered bells re-sound more clear-ly, forged of met-als bright and pure.

God blows breath of life and Spir-it— pre-lude in the morn-ing air.
we are tuned by dai-ly prac-tice, sea-soned by each les-son heard.
So our lives, re-fined by wis-dom, sound in ac-cents that en-dure.

We be-come God's liv-ing ves-sels: we, the flutes and pipes and reeds,
Skill-ful-ly the Spir-it plays us, fin-gers deft on fret and string,
God's own hand rings out the chang-es, strik-ing chords as yet un-known

ech-o-ing the Spir-it's mu-sic through the wit-ness of our deeds.
pluck-ing mel-o-dies of yearn-ing as our hearts res-pond and sing.
till a new earth fills with mu-sic rich and sweet as heav-en's own.

Text: Mary Louise Bringle, 2005. © 2005 GIA Publications, Inc.
Music: Charles Hubert Hastings Parry, 1897.

87 87D
RUSTINGTON

O Blessed Spring 114

1 O bless - ed spring, where word and sign em - brace us
2 Through sum - mer heat of youth - ful years, un - cer - tain
3 When au - tumn cools and youth is cold, when limbs their
4 As win - ter comes, as win - ters must, we breath our
5 Christ, ho - ly Vine, Christ, liv - ing Tree, be praised for

in - to Christ the Vine: here Christ en - joins each one to
faith, re - bel - lious tears, sus - tained by Christ's in - fus - ing
heav - y har - vest hold, then through us, warm, the Christ will
last, re - turn to dust; still held in Christ, our souls take
this blest mys - ter - y: that word and wa - ter thus re -

be a branch of this life - giv - ing Tree.
rain, the boughs will shout for joy a - gain.
move with gifts of beau - ty, wis - dom, love.
wing and trust the prom - ise of the spring.
vive and join us to your Tree of life.

Text: Susan Palo Cherwien, 1993, ©; admin. Augsburg Fortress.
Music: Melody English trad.; arr. Noel Tredinnick, 1982.
Arr. © 1982 The Jubilate Group, admin. Hope Publishing Co.

LM
O WALY, WALY

115 Long Before the Night

1 Long be-fore the night was born from
2 Long be-fore the grass spot-ted green the bare
3 Long be-fore a chain was forged from the
4 Long be-fore the name of a God was
5 Wake - ful our night slum - bers our

dark - ness, long be-fore the dawn rolled un -
hill - side, long be-fore a wing un -
hill - side, long be-fore a voice ut - tered
spo - ken, long be-fore a cross was
morn - ing, stub - born the grass sow - ing

stead - y from fire, long be-fore She
fold - ed to wind, long be-fore She
free - dom's cry, long be-fore She
nailed from a tree, long be-fore She
green wound - ed hills as we wrap our

Text: Carolyn McDade, 1988, 1995, ©.
Music: Carolyn McDade, 1988, ©; arr. David Kai, 1994, ©.

Irregular
THIS ANCIENT LOVE

116 One Thing I Ask

1 One thing I ask, one thing I seek,
2 Hear me, O Lord, hear me when I cry;

that I may dwell in your house, O Lord,
Lord, do not hide your face from me:

all of my days, all of my
you have been my strength, you have been my

life, that I may see you, Lord.
shield, and you will lift me

Text and music: Andy Park, 1987. © 1987 Mercy/Vineyard Publishing & Vineyard Songs.

Irregular
ONE THING I ASK

up.

One thing I ask, one thing I de - sire is to see you, is to see you.

117 Sometimes a Healing Word Is Comfort

1 Some-times a heal-ing word is com-fort: eas-ing the
2 Some-times a heal-ing word re-mem-bers: call-ing up
3 Some-times a heal-ing word is an-gry: giv-ing a
4 Some-times a heal-ing word takes chan-ces: go-ing where
5 Some-times a heal-ing word will lis-ten: hear-ing the

grieved or anx-ious heart, giv-ing as-sur-ance of our
days of joy or pain, let-ting the past re-new the
name to dis-con-tent, shin-ing a light on sin or
no one yet has been, fac-ing the dan-gers of the
voice-less in-to speech, let-ting the pat-tern of the

car - ing, trea-sur - ing each and ev'-ry part.
pres-ent, till hope can mend and move a-gain.
griev-ance, call-ing a peo-ple to re-pent.
des-ert, hop-ing for shel-ter at the inn.
sto-ry move us to learn what it can teach.

Text: Patrick Michaels, 1992.
Music: Curt Oliver, 1999. *Text and music © 2015 The Leupold Foundation.*

98 98 88
HEALING WORD

Come, break the si - lence! Let us tell the

Word that makes us free and well.

118 When We Are Living/*Pues si vivimos*

1 When we are liv-ing, we are in the Lord,
2 Each day al-lows us to de-cide for good,
3 Some-times we sor-row, oth-er times em-brace,
4 Till earth is o-ver may we al-ways know

and when we're dy-ing, we are in the Lord;
lov-ing and serv-ing as we know we should;
some-times we ques-tion ev-ery-thing we face;
love nev-er fails us: God has made it so.

for in our liv-ing and in our dy-ing
in thank-ful giv-ing, in hope-ful liv-ing,
yet in our yearn-ing is deep-er learn-ing;
Hard times will prove us, nev-er re-move us;

Text: St. 1, Anon.; st. 2–4, Roberto Escamilla, 1983; Eng. tr. John L. Bell, 2002.
Spanish text, st. 2–4 © Abingdon Press, admin. Music Service, Inc.
English trans. © 2002 WGRG c/o Iona Community, GIA Publications, Inc., agent.
Music: Melody Spanish trad.; arr. Michael Capon, 2017, ©.

10 10 10 10
SOMOS DEL SEÑOR

we be - long to God,   we be - long to God.
we be - long to God,   we be - long to God.
we be - long to God,   we be - long to God.
we be - long to God,   we be - long to God.

1 Pues si vivimos, para él vivimos;
   y si morimos, para él morimos.
   Sea que vivamos o que muramos,
   somos del Señor, somos del Señor.

2 En esta vida frutos hay que dar,
   y buenas obras hemos de ofrendar.
   Sea ya que demos o que recibamos,
   somos del Señor, somos del Señor.

3 En la tristeza y en el dolor,
   en la belleza y en el amor,
   sea que suframos o que gocemos,
   somos del Señor, somos del Señor.

4 En este mundo por doquier habrá
   gente que llora y sin consolar.
   Sea que ayudemos o que alimentemos,
   somos del Señor, somos del Señor.

119 You Are Before Me, Lord

Unison

1 You are be-fore me, Lord, you are be-hind,
2 Then from your Spir-it where, Lord, shall I go,
3 If I should take my flight in-to the dawn,
4 If I should say, "Let dark-ness cov-er me,
5 Search me, O God, search me and know my heart;

and o - ver me you have spread out your hand;
and from your pres - ence where, Lord, shall I fly?
if I should dwell on o - cean's far - thest shore,
and I shall hide with - in the veil of night,"
try me, O God, my mind and spir - it try;

Text: Psalm 139; para. Ian Pitt-Watson, 1973, 1989. © *Estate of Ian Pitt-Watson.*
Music: Alfred Morton Smith, 1941. © *Estate of Doris Wright Smith.*

10 10 10 10
SURSUM CORDA

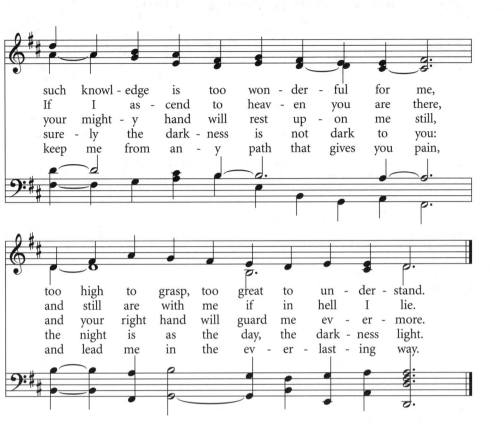

such   knowl - edge   is   too   won - der - ful   for   me,
If   I   as - cend   to   heav - en   you   are   there,
your   might - y   hand   will   rest   up - on   me   still,
sure - ly   the   dark - ness   is   not   dark   to   you:
keep   me   from   an - y   path   that   gives   you   pain,

too   high   to   grasp, too   great   to   un - der - stand.
and   still   are   with   me   if   in   hell   I   lie.
and   your   right   hand   will   guard   me   ev - er - more.
the   night   is   as   the   day,   the   dark - ness   light.
and   lead   me   in   the   ev - er - last - ing   way.

120 When We Are Tempted to Deny Your Son

1 When we are tempt - ted to de - ny your
2 When we are tempt - ted to be - tray your
3 When we for - get the cross that held your
4 When doubt ob - scures the vic - tory of your

Son be - cause we fear the an - ger of the
Son be - cause he leads us in a hard - er
Son and would a - void the bur - den of this
Son and faith is weak and all re - solve has

world, and we are few who bear the
way, and makes de - mands we do not
life, the cry for jus - tice, and an
fled, help us to know him ris - en

in - sults hurled: your will, O God, be done.
want to pay: your will, O God, be done.
end to strife: your will, O God, be done.
from the dead: your will, O God, be done.

Text: David W. Romig, 1965. © 1972 Westminster Press.
Music: J. Harold Moyer, 1965.
Music © 1969 Faith and Life Press/Mennonite Publishing House, admin. MennoMedia Inc.

10 10 10 6
FAITH

Like a Mother Who Has Borne Us 121

D   G   A   D

1 Like a moth - er who has borne us, held us
2 Like a fa - ther who has taught us, grasped our
3 Though as chil - dren we have wan - dered, placed our
4 When we of - fer food and com - fort, grasp our

A   D   A   Bm   G   Em

close in her de - light, fed us free - ly from her
hand and been our guide, lift - ed us and healed our
trust in power and might, left be - hind our broth - ers,
neigh - bour's hand in love, tread the path of peace and

Bm   A   G   D   A   D

bod - y, God has called us in - to life.
sor - rows, God has walked with us in life.
sis - ters, God still calls us in - to life.
jus - tice, God still walks with us in life.

Text: Daniel Bechtel, 1986, ©.
Music: William P. Rowan, 1992. © 1993 Selah Publishing Co., Inc.

87 87
AUSTIN

TRUST

122 Before the Throne of God Above

1 Be - fore the throne of God a - bove I have a
2 When Sa - tan tempts me to de - spair, and tells me
3 Be - hold him there! the ris - en Lamb! my per - fect,

strong, a per - fect plea: a great High Priest, whose name is
of the guilt with - in, up - ward I look, and see him
spot - less Right-eous - ness, the great un - change - a - ble I

Love, who ev - er lives and pleads for me. My name is
there who made an end of all my sin. Be - cause the
AM, the King of glo - ry and of grace! One with my

Text: Charitie Lees Bancroft, 1863.
Music: Vikki Cook, 1997.
Music © 1997 Sovereign Grace Worship, admin. EMI CMG Publishing.

LMD with repeat
BEFORE THE THRONE

123 Don't Be Afraid

Don't be a-fraid. My love is strong-er, my love is strong-er than your fear. Don't be a-fraid. My love is strong-er and I have prom-ised, prom-ised to be al - ways near.

Text and music: John L. Bell, 1995.
© 1995 WGRG c/o Iona Community, GIA Publications, Inc., agent.

Irregular

In the Lord I'll Be Ever Thankful

In the Lord I'll be ev - er thank - ful, in the Lord I will re - joice! Look to God, do not be a - fraid. Lift up your voic - es, the Lord is near. Lift up your voic - es, the Lord is near.

Text: Taizé Community, 1986.
Music: Jacques Berthier, 1986.
© 1991 Les Presses de Taizé, GIA Publications, Inc., agent.

Irregular
IN THE LORD I'LL BE EVER THANKFUL

125 *Mungu ni Mwema*/Know That God Is Good

Text and music: Democratic Republic of Congo; music arr. Edo Bumba, 1997, ©;
French tr. David Fines, 2005, ©.

Like a Rock

Actions for "Like a Rock":

Like a rock: Extend both forearms upward, palms facing down in one movement.

Like the starry night sky: Wiggle fingers while slowly raising arms to head height.

Like the sun: Extend one foream, palm up. With palm down, slowly extend the other hand 6" over the first arm, arcing up at the end, so the palm is facing away from the body.

Like the river: Leave the first forearm as before. Other hand makes a "swimming" motion close to it, by weaving it gently in handshake position.

Evermore: End with "God's hug"—crossing arms over chest, hands to shoulders.

Text: Keri K. Wehlander, 1998, ©.
Music: Linnea Good, 1999, ©.

Irregular
LIKE A ROCK

127 A Voice Was Heard in Ramah

1 A voice was heard in Ra - mah that could not be con-
2 O God, we hear the cry - ing for lit - tle ones of
3 When - ev - er one is weep - ing, the whole world suf - fers,
4 O Prince of Peace, you lead us in ways of truth and

soled, as Ra - chel wept for chil - dren she
yours; for man - y still are dy - ing in
too. Yet, Je - sus, as we serve them, we're
grace. May we be brave to prac - tice your

could no long - er hold. For Her - od ruled the
con - flicts and in wars. In ev - ery trou - bled
al - so serv - ing you. So may we not ig -
peace in ev - ery place, to love each fear - filled

Text: Carolyn Winfrey Gillette, 2004, ©.
Music: Melody Welsh trad.; *Hymnau a Thonau*, 1865;
harm. *The English Hymnal*, 1906, © Oxford University Press.

76 76D
LLANGLOFFAN

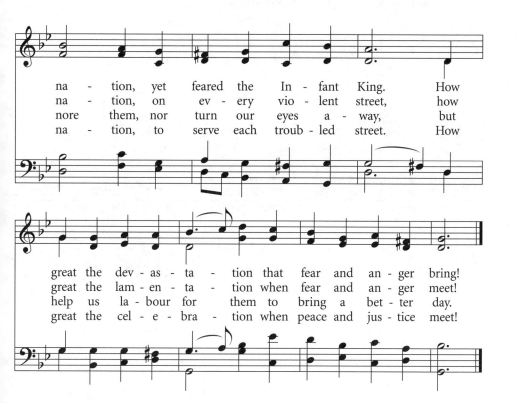

na - tion, yet feared the In - fant King. How
na - tion, on ev - ery vio - lent street, how
nore them, nor turn our eyes a - way, but
na - tion, to serve each troub - led street. How

great the dev - as - ta - tion that fear and an - ger bring!
great the lam - en - ta - tion when fear and an - ger meet!
help us la - bour for them to bring a bet - ter day.
great the cel - e - bra - tion when peace and jus - tice meet!

128 Jesus Christ Is Waiting

1 Je - sus Christ is wait - ing, wait - ing in the streets;
2 Je - sus Christ is rag - ing, rag - ing in the streets,
3 Je - sus Christ is heal - ing, heal - ing in the streets,
4 Je - sus Christ is danc - ing, danc - ing in the streets,
5 Je - sus Christ is call - ing, call - ing in the streets,

no one is his neigh - bour, all a - lone he eats.
where in - jus - tice spi - rals and real hope re - treats.
cur - ing those who suf - fer, touch-ing those he greets.
where each sign of ha - tred he, with love, de - feats.
"Who will join my jour - ney? I will guide their feet."

Text: John L. Bell and Graham Maule, 1984.
Music: Melody French trad., harm. John L. Bell.
Text and harm. © 1988 WGRG c/o Iona Community, GIA Publications, Inc., agent.

11 11 11 10
NOËL NOUVELET

Lis - ten, Lord Je - sus, I am lone - ly too.
Lis - ten, Lord Je - sus, I am an - gry too.
Lis - ten, Lord Je - sus, I have pit - y too.
Lis - ten, Lord Je - sus, I should tri - umph too.
Lis - ten, Lord Je - sus, let my fears be few.

Make me, friend or stran - ger, fit to wait on you.
In the King - dom's caus - es, let me rage with you.
Let my care be ac - tive, heal - ing just like you.
On sus - pi - cion's grave - yard, let me dance with you.
Walk one step be - fore me; I will fol - low you.

129 Welcome, Jesus, You Are Welcome

1 Wel - come, Je - sus, you are wel - come in this
2 Wel - come, Je - sus, you are wel - come in the
3 Wel - come, Je - sus, you are wel - come with the
4 Wel - come, Je - sus, you are wel - come; let your

world made hard by fear; lov - ing reach us,
ghet - tos we have made; give the tat - tered,
wealth - y and the poor; give the bro - ken
lov - ing light ap - pear. In our see - ing,

liv - ing teach us, Je - sus, you are wel - come here.
bruised and bat - tered win - ter shel - ter, sum - mer shade.
love un - spo - ken, o - pen wide each pris - on door.
in our be - ing, Je - sus, you are wel - come here.

Text and music: Daniel Charles Damon, 1992, rev. 2004. © 2005 Hope Publishing Co.   87 87
SWEETWATER

Freedom Is Coming 130

Text and music: South Africa. © 1984, *Peace of Music Publishing AB,*
admin. by Walton Music Corp., a division of GIA Publications, Inc.

Irregular
FREEDOM IS COMING

131 Live into Hope

1. Live in - to hope of cap - tives freed,
2. Live in - to hope! The blind shall see
3. Live in - to hope of lib - er - ty,
4. Live in - to hope of cap - tives freed

of sight re - gained, the end of greed.
with in - sight and with clar - i - ty,
the right to speak, the right to be,
from chains of fear or want or greed.

The poor shall be the first to see
re - mov - ing shades of pride and fear,
the right to have one's dai - ly bread,
God now pro - claims our full re - lease

the year of God's own ju - bi - lee!
a vis - ion of our God brought near.
to hear God's word and thus be fed.
to faith and hope and joy and peace.

Text: Jane Parker Huber, 1976, alt., ©. *Used by permission of Westminster/John Knox Press.*
Music: Thom Mitchell, ©.

LM
LIVE INTO HOPE
Alt. tune TRURO.

Sisters, Let Us Walk Together 132

1 Sisters, let us walk together, sharing sadness, loss and grief. We will move through pain to wholeness; brokenness transformed to peace.

2 Brothers, let us work together, seeking justice, healing shame. Filled with hope, embued with courage, ev'ry violence we will name.

3 People, let us love together, joining spirits, linking hands. We are God's unique creation; clothed with dignity we'll stand.

May be sung as a two- or three-part round.

Text and music: Judith Snowdon, 2004, ©.

87 87
SISTERS LET US WALK

133 When Hands Reach Out Beyond Divides

1 When hands reach out be - yond di - vides and
2 When fear no long - er guides our steps and
3 When race and creed blind us no more, a

hope is tru - ly found, each chain of hate will
days of war are done, God's dream for all shall
neigh - bour's face we'll see, and we shall dance the

fall a - way and bells of peace shall sound, and
live a - new, our hearts will heal as one, our
whole world round, for love will set us free, for

Text: Keri K. Wehlander, 2005, ©.
Music: Melody anon., *Southern Harmony*, 1854; arr. Melva Treffinger Graham, 2006, ©.

CMD
SALEM

bells of peace, of peace shall sound, and
hearts will heal, will heal as one, our
love, yes love will set us free, for

bells of peace shall sound, each chain of hate will
hearts will heal as one, God's dream for all shall
love will set us free, and we shall dance the

fall a - way and bells of peace shall sound.
live a - new, our hearts will heal as one.
whole world round, for love will set us free.

134 When the Hungry Who Have Nothing

1 When the hun-gry who have noth-ing share with
2 When the suf-fering find their com-fort in our
3 When a spir-it of re-joic-ing fills us
4 When true good-ness makes each home a hal-lowed

stran-gers; when the thirst-y give us
car-ing; when their hope springs from a
deep-ly; when the truth rings from our
shel-ter; when the war-torn of-fer

drink, ask-ing no price; when in
hope that nev-er tires; when all
lips, stron-ger than lies; when we
peace, bless-ed and wise; when each

Text and music: José Antonio Olivar and Miguel Manzano, 1971; arr. Alvin Schutmaat, 1971. 12 11 12 11 11
Eng. tr. Mary Louise Bringle, 2005; © 1971 José Antonio Olivar and Miguel Manzano;   EL CAMINO
admin. OCP Publications.

weak-ness,   we still strength-en   one an - oth - er:
ha - tred   melts in   em - bers   of our   lov - ing:
hon - our   Christ's ex - am - ple   to live   sim - ply:
stran - ger   is our   broth - er   or our   sis - ter:

God goes with us   on the path - ways of our lives.

God goes with us   on the path - ways of our lives.

135 Walking and Wheeling

Walk - ing and wheel - ing, stand - ing and kneel - ing, let them all pro - phe - sy.

Speak - ing and hear - ing, see - ing and fear - ing, let them all pro - phe - sy.

Think - ing and feel - ing, lov - ing and heal - ing, let them all pro - phe - sy.

Do - ing and dar - ing, for - ward be far - ing, let them all pro - phe - sy!

May be sung as a four-part round.

Text: William Whitla, 2003, ©.
Music: Becca Whitla, 2004, ©.

When Our Song Says Peace 136

1 When our song says peace and the world says war, we will
2 When our song says free and the world says bound, we will
3 When our song says home and the world says lost, we will

sing de-spite the world. We will trust the song, for we sing of God
sing de-spite the world. We will trust the song, for we sing of God
sing de-spite the world. We will trust the song, for we sing of God

who breaks the spear and sword and stills the storm of war.
who o-pens pris-on doors and sets the cap-tive free.
who brings us home at last and gives a song to all.

Text: Richard Leach, 1995. © 1995 Selah Publishing Co., Inc.
Music: Thomas Pavlechko, 2003. © 2003 Augsburg Fortress.

10 7 10 6 6
JENKINS

MISSION

137 Called to Faith

1 Called to faith, your peo - ple gath - er, Christ our broth - er,
2 Called to hope, your peo - ple serve you as they reach out
3 Called to love, your peo - ple chal - lenge all that si - lenc -

in your name, know - ing need of one an - oth - er,
through your grace, seek - ing out your mis - sion's pur - pose,
es your song: pre - ju - dice and greed and mal - ice,

fac - es dif - ferent, hearts the same, grow - ing in your
be - ing Christ in ev - ery place, work - ing for sha -
weak ex - ploit - ed by the strong. Serv - ing Je - sus

Text: Ellen Clark-King, 2007, ©.
Music: William Penfro Rowlands, 1905.

87 87D
BLAENWERN

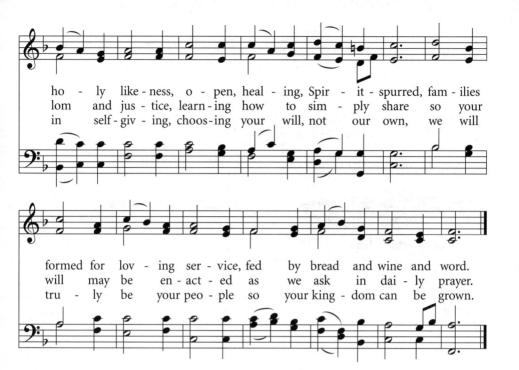

ho - ly like - ness, o - pen, heal - ing, Spir - it - spurred, fam - ilies
lom and jus - tice, learn - ing how to sim - ply share so your
in self - giv - ing, choos - ing your will, not our own, we will

formed for lov - ing ser - vice, fed by bread and wine and word.
will may be en - act - ed as we ask in dai - ly prayer.
tru - ly be your peo - ple so your king - dom can be grown.

138 Loving Church, I Hear Your Praises

1 Lov-ing church, I hear your prais - es, your faith-ful wor - ship here to - day. To make it more than just sweet phras - es, let your life my love o - bey. Will you help me build my king - dom? Will you meet me in the street? I will be there wait - ing for you in

2 Do your neigh - bours sense I love them? I've chos - en you to let them know. I have man - y lone - ly child - ren; it's to them that you must go. Will you help me feed the hun - gry? Will you gen - tly lift the weak? I am ask - ing you: rise up to - day, be -

Text and music: Gail Poulsen and Linda Lensink, 2014, ©.

Irregular
Wherever You Go

I'm Gonna Live So God Can Use Me

1 I'm gon-na live so (live so) God can use me
2 I'm gon-na work so (work so) God can use me
3 I'm gon-na pray so (pray so) God can use me
4 I'm gon-na sing so (sing so) God can use me

an - y - where, Lord, an - y - time! I'm gon-na
an - y - where, Lord, an - y - time! I'm gon-na
an - y - where, Lord, an - y - time! I'm gon-na
an - y - where, Lord, an - y - time! I'm gon-na
(an - y - time!)

live so (live so) God can use me an - y -
work so (work so) God can use me an - y -
pray so (pray so) God can use me an - y -
sing so (sing so) God can use me an - y -

where, Lord, an - y - time!
where, Lord, an - y - time!
where, Lord, an - y - time!
where, Lord, an - y - time!
(my Lord,) (an - y - time!)

Text: African-American spiritual.
Music: African-American spiritual; arr. Wendell P. Whalum, 1984.
  Arr. © Estate of Wendell P. Whalum.

Irregular
I'M GONNA LIVE

140 Create within Me a Clean Heart

Ostinato: Chimes or Bells

*Sopranos and tenors sing "Create in me..."
Altos and basses sing "Adoramus Domine."
When sung in four-part harmony, for the
first singing the sopranos may sing the text
while the other parts are hummed. Then
the tenors may join and subsequently altos
and basses sing the Latin text.*

Create with-in me a clean heart, O God;

A - do - ra - mus, Do - mi - ne,

place at my cen - tre a new and right spir - it.

quo - ni - am tu so - lus sanc - tus.

Since you want truth in my in - ner-most be - ing,

A - do - ra - mus, Do - mi - ne,

teach me your wis - dom in my sec - ret heart.

quo - ni - am tu so - lus sanc - tus.

Text and melody: Alison Adam, 2001, ©. Music arr. John L. Bell, 2001.
Arr. © 2001 WGRG c/o Iona Community, GIA Publications, Inc., agent.

10 11 11 10
CLEAN HEART

From the Depths of Sin and Sadness   141

1 From the depths of sin and sad - ness
2 If you, Lord, re - cord our sin - ning,
3 For the Lord my heart is wait - ing;

I have called un - to the Lord.
who could then be - fore you stand?
for God's word I hope and wait.

Be not deaf to my poor plead - ing. In your
But with you there is for - give - ness. You shall
More than watch - ers wait for sun - rise I am

mer - cy, hear my voice.
ev - er be re - vered.
wait - ing for the Lord.

Text: Willard F. Jabusch, 1966, ©, *admin. OCP Publications.*
Music: Melody Russian trad.; alto line Harris J. Loewen, 1988, ©;
   tenor and bass lines Kenneth Hull, 2019, ©.

87 87 with repeat
FROM THE DEPTHS

142 I Did Not Hear the Mother's Cry

Unison

1 I did not hear the moth-er's cry, though hun-ger caused her
2 I did not go to ease the stress of some-one trapped in
3 I did not speak where words have pow'r, so e - vil reigned that
4 I did not see the clouds of war, nor saw what grief might

child to die. Lord, may I sense a neigh-bour's fear: where
will - ful - ness; but feet as well as tongues can talk: where
shame - ful hour. Lord, use my voice to help the weak: where
be in store. Now more per - cep - tive I would be: where

I've been deaf, pray, help me hear.
I've been lame, Lord, help me walk.
I've been si - lent, help me speak.
I've been blind, Lord, help me see.

Text: Rae E. Whitney, 1993. © 1993 Selah Publishing Co., Inc.
Music: Thomas Pavlechko, 2002. © 2005 Selah Publishing Co., Inc.

LM
WILLIAMS

If I Have Been the Source of Pain 143

Text: Sara M. De Hall, based on a text by C. M. Battersby; English tr. Janet W. May, 1992.
English tr. © 1992 The Pilgrim Press.
Music: Pablo Sosa, 1988. © 1988 GIA Publications, Inc.

10 10 10 4
CAMACUÁ

144 *Loe de Ísá*/Jesus Knows the Inmost Heart

Harmony

Bm　Em　　　D　G　　Am⁷　Bm⁷　Em　*Fine*

Lo - e de Í - sá ust - áz　hál da zra tá go - rí.
Je - sus knows the in - most heart—　no - thing can be hid - den.

Unison Em　　Bm　　Am　　　　Em　　C

1 This our sin - ful hearts re - quire:　flame of God's re -
2 Je - sus knows our deep - est fears,　know the pain of
3 When our lives are in his hand　no - thing can his
4 So our faith will be re - stored　by the word of

Am　Em/G　Em　Em⁷　Am　D⁷

fin - ing fire work - ing in us day by day
hid - den tears. By his words of love and peace
work with - stand; his for - give - ness sets us free,
Christ our Lord; for the warmth his love im - parts

Em　　　　　　Am⁷　Bm⁷　Em　*D.C.*

till the dross is burned a - way.
ev - ery heart can find re - lease.
saves us for e - ter - ni - ty.
melts the ver - y hard - est hearts.

Text: Pashto hymn (Pakistan); trans. Alison Blenkinsop, 1995, ©.
Music: Unknown; arr. Geoff Weaver, 1995.
Music arr. © 1995 The Jubilate Group, admin. Hope Publishing Co.

77 77 with refrain
LOE DE ISA

Tama ngakau marie/Son of God 145

1 Ta - ma nga - kau ma - ri - e, ta - ma
1 Son of God, whose heart is peace, Son of
2 Take a - way our sin - ful - ness, e - vil
3 Warm our hearts to love you, Lord, you who

a t'A - tu - a, te - nei to - nu
God, most ho - ly, to your pres - ence
that im - pris - ons us. Free us from what
died to save us. Gath - er us with -

ma - tou, a - ro - hai - na mai.
we have come; give us now your love.
trou - bles us; give our souls re - lease.
in your arms, Je - sus, on this day.

2 *Murua ra nga hara:*
   wetekina mai,
   enei here kino,
   whakararu nei.

3 *Homai he aroha*
   mou i mate nei
   tenei ra, e Ihu
   takina i koe.

Text: Maori trad.; para. Shirley Erena Murray. *Para. © 1990, 2000 Christian Conference of Asia,*
   admin. GIA Publications, Inc.
Music: Maori trad. melody.

76 75
TAMA NGAKAU MARIE

146 While I Keep Silence

1 While I keep si - lence, si - lence,
2 My thirst - ing spir - it, spir - it,
3 All you who wan - der, wan - der,

si - lence in my flesh, my breath and bod - y
spir - it wastes a - way; I with - er in the
wan - der with - out hope, who know your man - y

fail. My sins grow bit - ter, bit - ter,
sun. But as I'm turn - ing, turn - ing,
sins, seek out the Sav - iour, Sav - iour,

bit - ter in my mouth. My bones re - turn to
turn - ing toward the night, you split the si - lent
Sav - iour while he's found; he hides you in his

dust. O God, I groan both day and
skies. O God, I stand be - neath the
hand. O God, you hear us day and

night be - neath your heav - y hand.
rain, be - neath the cleans - ing rain.
night; re - store us by your hand.

These notes may be hummed throughout the hymn, beginning at these places.

Text: David Wright, 2005; based on Psalm 32.3-5, ©.
Music: James E. Clemens, 2005, ©.

Irregular
SILENCE

I Am the World's True Light/*Yo soy la luz* 147

1 C   G

I am the world's true light. If you will fol - low
Yo soy la luz del mun - do. El que me si - ga ten -

C   F

me, your life will re - flect my bright - ness and
drá ta luz que la da la vi - da. Y

G7   C   **2** C   G

you'll nev - er walk in the night. A - le - lu - ya,
nun - ca an - da - rá en la os - cu - ri - dad.

C   F   G7

a - le - lu - ya, a - le - lu - ya, a - le -

C   **3** C   G7

lu! La, la, la, la, la, la. God is our light, God is our peace,
Dios es la luz, Dios es la paz,

C

God is our love. God is our light,
Dios es a - mor. Dios es la luz,

F   G7   C

God is our peace, God is our love.
Dios es la paz, Dios es a - mor.

Text and music: Attrib. Rudolfo Ascencio; English tr. C. Michael Hawn, 1999.   Irregular
English tr. © 1999 Choristers Guild.

148 As Tender As a Mother Hen

1 As ten-der as a moth-er hen who spreads her
2 Cou-ra-geous as a moth-er bear who guards her
3 A phoe-nix ris-ing from the flames, a moth-er

wings to shield her brood, Christ Je-sus stretch-es out his
young from dan-ger's path, Christ Je-sus wields his zeal-ous
ea - gle, soar-ing high, Christ Je-sus lifts the wear-y

arms and sheds his life as ho-ly food.
love and shows the gift of right-ful wrath.
world and con-qers death for all who die.

Text: Mary Louise Bringle, 2003.
Music: Carl F. Schalk, 1981. Text © 2006 and music © 1981 GIA Publications, Inc.

88 88 88 87
MARVEL

We seek his pat - tern in our hearts a - mazed by
We heed his call, op - pos - ing pow'rs that thwart the
In him, we find our strength re - newed and, mount - ing

such un - self - ish grace, and tend the chil - dren
cause of life and health, and strive to reach the
up on fledg - ling wings, we rise to share the

of the world in whom we see God's face.
proph - ets' dreams to build God's Com - mon - wealth.
gos - pel hope that res - ur - rec - tion brings!

149 Christ Jesus Lord from Heav'n Above

1 Christ Jesus Lord from heav'n above, cum dung to all a
2 You died on Cal-v'ry for our sake, cum dung to all a
3 O rid us of all care and woe, cum dung to all a
4 Cum dung, Lord, an' a go no more, cum dung to all a

we; O fill us with your might-y love, cum dung to all a
we; a-mend-ments for our sins you make, cum dung to all a
we; and put in place your heaven-ly glow, cum dung to all a
we; cum dung an' stay up-on dis shore, cum dung to all a

we; We be not wor-thy of your grace, cum dung to all a we;
we; shine down on us your ra-diant light, cum dung to all a we;
we; come in all power and maj-es-ty, cum dung to all a we;
we. Yes, cum dung, Lord, please go no more, cum dung to all a we.

but help us, Lord, to see your face, cum dung to all a we.
en-light-en our sins' dark-est night, cum dung to all a we.
bring us sal-va-tion, make us free, cum dung to all a we.
O cum dung, Lord, for ev-er-more, cum dung to all a we.

Text and melody: Everton Joseph; harm. Noel Dexter.
© 1958 Caribbean Conference of Churches.

85 85 with refrain
CUM DUNG

Refrain

Cum dung, Je - sus, cum dung, cum dung,

cum dung to all a we; O Lord

Je - sus, cum dung to all a we.

150 Christ Sophia

1 Christ So - phi - a, Child of Wis - dom: danc - ing in our
2 Broth - er Je - sus, Child of Mar - y: walk - ing with us
3 God in - car - nate, our true moth - er, birth - ing us to

deep - est dreams, call - ing us to love un - bound - ed,
on life's way, show - ing us God's hum - ble king - dom,
joy and pain, show - ing us the steps to dance to,

dar - ing us to God's ex - tremes— peace and gen - tle -
shar - ing both dark night and day, break - ing through death's
lov - ing us to life a - gain: grow us in - to

Text: Ellen Clark-King, 2011, ©.
Music: John Hughes, 1907.

87 87 87 with repeat
CWM RHONDDA

ness   and jus - tice,   king - dom val - ues, wis - dom's
seem - ing end - ing   in - to new life's dawn - ing
your   true im - age   as   we strive for your love's

themes,   king - dom val - ues,   wis - dom's themes,
ray,   in - to new   life's   dawn - ing ray.
reign,   as   we strive for   your   love's reign.

151 Jesus Before Me

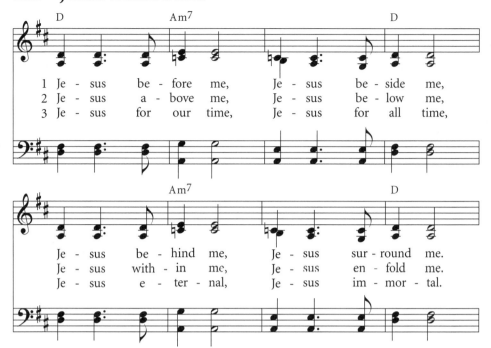

1 Je - sus be - fore me, Je - sus be - side me,
2 Je - sus a - bove me, Je - sus be - low me,
3 Je - sus for our time, Je - sus for all time,

Je - sus be - hind me, Je - sus sur - round me.
Je - sus with - in me, Je - sus en - fold me.
Je - sus e - ter - nal, Je - sus im - mor - tal.

Text and music: Andy Moss, 2005, ©.

10 10 8 8
CIRCLE ME, LORD

Refrain

Cir – cle me, Lord,   cir – cle me, Lord,

Cir – – – cle me, cir – – – cle me,

Cir – cle me, Lord,   cir – cle me, Lord,

F   Gsus⁴   G   Gm   Asus⁴   A

all   of   my   days,   cir – cle   me,   Lord.

Am   Dm⁷   Gsus⁴   G   Gm   Am   Dm

152 Jesus, the Perfect Picture

1 Je - sus, the per - fect pic - ture of the un - seen God;
2 Vic - tor, o - ver sin and death you tri - umphed.

Mak - er of things we can - not com - pre - hend;
First - born, you've shown us life be - yond the grave.

Wis - dom, the earth dis - plays your strength and beau - ty.
Bride - groom, we long for you in ex - pec - ta - tion.

Sov - ereign, yes, ev - ery throne knows you are God.
Je - sus, your church re - joic - es to pro - claim:

Text: Matthew Westerholm, 1999.
Music: Matthew Westerholm, 1999; arr. Greg Scheer.
Text and music © 1999 Matthew Westerholm.

Irregular
THE FIRST PLACE

Refrain

Ev-ery inch of this u - ni-verse be-longs to you, O Christ, for through

you and for you it was made. Your cre - a - tion en-dures by the

or-der of your hand, so you must have in all things the first

place.

153 *Kwake Yesu nasimama*/Here on Jesus Christ

Refrain

Swahili: Kwa-ke Ye-su na-si-ma-ma, ndi-ye mwam-ba ni
English: Here on Je-sus Christ I will stand. He's the sol-id rock

___ sa-la-ma. Ndi-ye mwam-ba ni sa-la-ma, ndi-ye
___ of my life. He's the sol-id rock of my life. He's the

Fine

mwam-ba ni sa-la-ma.
sol-id rock of my life.

1 There's no oth-er place I can
2 It is not the work of my
3 When my days on this earth are

Text: Kenyan hymn; English adapt. Greg Scheer, 2007. *Text © 2007 East Africa Annual Conference, admin. General Board of Global Ministries t/a GBGMusik. English adapt.© 2007 Greg Scheer, admin. General Board of Global Ministries t/a/ GBGMusik.*
Music: Kenyan melody; arr. Greg Scheer, 2007.
    Arr. © 2007 Greg Scheer, admin. General Board of Global Ministries t/a/GBGMusik.

LM

KWAKE YESU NASIMAMA

hide   till   the   storm   that rag - es sub - sides. My voice
hands   that   has   washed a - way   all my   sins. I'm re -
done,   and   I   stand   at God's ho - ly   throne, my   heart

cries   to   God   from the   flood,   and   I'm
deemed, and   all   of   my   days   Je - sus
will   not   have   an - y   fear;   in   Christ's

saved   be - cause   of   his   blood.
Christ   will be   my   heart's praise.
right - eous - ness   I   am   here.

154 Jesus, Our Mighty Lord

1 Je - sus, our might - y Lord, our strength in sad - ness,
the Fa - ther's con - quering Word, true source of glad - ness—
your name we glo - ri - fy, O Je - sus throned on
high: you gave your-self to die for our sal - va - tion.

2 Good shep - herd of your sheep, your own de - fend - ing,
in love your child - ren keep to life un - end - ing.
You are your-self the way: lead us then day by
day in your own steps, we pray, O Lord most ho - ly.

3 Glo - rious their life who sing, with glad thanks-giv - ing,
true hymns to Christ the King in all their liv - ing:
all who con - fess his name, come then with hearts a -
flame, the God of peace ac - claim as Lord and Sav - iour.

Text: Clement of Alexandria, late 2nd or early 3rd cent.; para. F. Bland Tucker.
Para. © The Church Pension Fund.
Music: Melody English trad.; adapt. Ralph Vaughan Williams, 1906.
Music © Oxford University Press.

11 11 12 11
MONK'S GATE

Heri ni jina/Blessed Be the Name 155

He - ri ni ji - na, he - ri ni ji - na, he - ri ni ji - na la Ye -
Bless-ed be the name, bless-ed be the name, bless - ed be the name, Je - sus'

su. He - ri - ni - ji - na, he - ri ni ji - na,
name. Bless - ed be the name, bless - ed be the name,

he - ri ni ji - na la Ye - su. (A - mi - ni!)
bless - ed be the name, Je - sus' name. (Be - lieve!)

Al - le - lu - ya, al - le - lu - ya.
Al - le - lu - ia, al - le - lu - ia.

He - ri - ni - ji - na la Ye - su. (A - mi - ni!) Al - le - lu - ya,
Bless-ed be the name, Je - sus' name. (Be-lieve!) Al - le - lu - ia,

al - le - lu - ya. He - ri ni ji - na la Ye - su.
al - le - lu - ia. Bless-ed be the name, Je - sus' name.

Text: As taught by Deogratias Mahamba.
Music: East African trad.; arr. Mark Sedio, 2003. Arr. © 2003 Augsburg Fortress.

558D 448D
HERI NI JINA

156 I Heard the Voice of Jesus Calling

Refrain

I hear the voice of Je-sus call-ing; here's what he said to me:

1 If you don't let me wash your feet, I can't your
2 All that you do for the least of these— that's what you
3 If you have ears to hear, then hear; if you have
4 Your deep-est prayer I will ful - fill where two or

Sav - iour be; no, I can't your Sav - iour be.
do to me; yes, that's what you do to me.
eyes, then see; oh, if you have eyes, then see.
three a - gree; yes, where two or three a - gree.

5 I've come that you may know the truth—
   that's what will set you free; yes,
   that's what will set you free.

6 This is my body, given for you—
   why don't you taste and see? Oh,
   why don't you taste and see?

7 Believe in me and you will live
   through all eternity; yes,
   through all eternity.

Text and melody: John L. Bell, 2008.
© 2008 WGRG c/o Iona Community, GIA Publications, Inc., agent.

86 86 6
LOUISE

As the Wind Song Through the Trees 157

1 As the wind song through the trees, as the stir - ring of the breeze, so it is with the Spir - it of God. As the

2 As the rain - bow af - ter rain, as the hope born a - gain, so it is with the Spir - it of God. As the

Text: Shirley Erena Murray, 2004.
Music: Lim Swee Hong, 2004. *Text and music © 2005 Hope Publishing Co.*

Irregular
WAIRUA TAPU

life,   bring-ing power   to the world,   as the
gifts,   bring-ing love   to the world,   as the

Em   Bm   Am   D

danc - ing tongues of fire,   as the soul's most deep de - sire,   so it
ris - ing   of   the yeast,   as the wine at   the   feast,   so it

Em   Em/D   C   G/B

is   with   the   Spir - it   of   God.
is   with   the   Spir - it   of   God.

Am⁷   D   G   C/G   G

158 Bring Us Love

Bring us love, bring us love, bring us
joy, bring us joy, bring us peace by your
Spir-it, Lord, bring us love and joy and peace.
Bring us pa-tience, bring us pa-tience, bring us
kind-ness, bring us kind-ness, bring us good-ness by your
Spir-it, Lord, bring us love and joy and peace.
Bring us faith-ful-ness, bring us faith-ful-ness, bring us hu-
mil-it-y, bring us hu-mil-it-y, bring us will-pow-er by your
Spir-it, Lord, bring us love and joy and peace.

Text and music: Larry Campbell, 2010, ©.

Irregular
BY YOUR SPIRIT

Come, O Holy Spirit/*Wa wa wa Emimimo* 159

Come, O Holy Spir-it come;
Wa wa wa E-mi-mi-mo;

Ho-ly Spir-it, come.
E-mi-o-lo-ye.

Come, al-might-y Spir-it, come;
Wa wa wa A-lag-ba-ra;

al-might-y Spir-it, come.
A-log-ba-ra-me-ta.

Come, come, come.
Wa-o, wa-o, wa-o.

O Spir-it, come.
E-mi-mi-mo.

Text: Yoruba trad., © *The Church of the Lord (Aladura)*; Eng. para. I-to Loh, 1986.
Music: Yoruba trad., © *The Church of the Lord (Aladura)* transcr. *taught by Samuel Solanke
and English paraphrase* © 1986 WCC and the Asian Institute for Liturgy and Music.

Irregular
WA EMIMIMO

160 Spirit, Open My Heart

Refrain

Spir-it, o-pen my heart to the joy and pain of liv-ing. As you love may I love, in re-ceiv-ing and in giv-ing. Spir-it, o-pen my heart.

Text: Ruth Duck, 1994. © *1996 The Pilgrim Press.*
Music: Melody Irish trad.; arr. Alfred V. Fedak, 2011, alt., ©.

Irregular
WILD MOUNTAIN THYME

1 God, re - place my ston - y heart with a heart that's
2 Write your love up - on my heart as my law, my
3 May I weep with those who weep share the joy of

kind and ten - der. All my cold - ness and
goal, my sto - ry. In each thought, word, and
sis - ter, broth - er. In the wel - come of

to refrain

fear to your grace I now sur - ren - der.
deed, may my liv - ing bring you glo - ry.
Christ, may we wel - come one an - oth - er.

161 Holy Spirit, Come to Us/*Veni Sancte Spiritus*

Ho-ly Spir-it, come to us, kin-dle in us the fire of your love.
Ve - ni San-cte Spir - i - tus, tu - i a-mo-ris i - gnem ac - cen - de.

Ho - ly Spir - it, come to us. Ho - ly Spir - it, come to us.
Ve - ni San - cte Spir - i - tus, ve - ni San - cte Spir - i - tus.

Text: Taizé Community.
Music: Jacques Berthier.
Text and music ©1998 Les Presses de Taizé, GIA Publications, Inc., agent.

Irregular
TUI AMORIS IGNEM

The Holy Spirit Came to Me 162

1 The Ho - ly Spir - it came to me: she
2 The Ho - ly Spir - it came to me: she
3 The Ho - ly Spir - it came to me: and
4 The Ho - ly Spir - it came to me: she
5 The Ho - ly Spir - it came to me: she
6 The Ho - ly Spir - it comes to me in

fed and clothed me, worked and played; she showed me how to
taught me mu - sic of the soul; she showed how time and
soon be - came a trust - ed friend; though springs and win - ters
loved me as I was but said she loved me more, and
knew my worth and saw my need; she lift - ed lids, she
ev - 'ry time, on ev - 'ry side; wher - ev - er I may

look and see the world, and not to be a - fraid.
sound and touch com - bine to make a ra - diant whole.
come and go her con - stant love will nev - er end.
sought to bring to life the me I'd left for dead.
op - ened doors; we swept the house and plant - ed seeds.
turn she is al - read - y there: my friend and guide.

Text: Patrick Michaels, 1990, ©.
Music: David Buley, 2016. © 2016 Rublemusic.

LM
NEPAWHIN

163 We Sing a Love That Sets All People Free

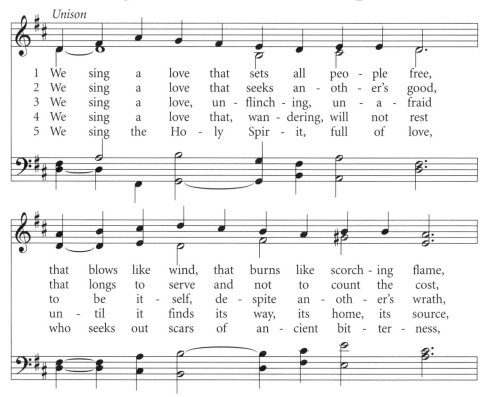

Unison

1 We sing a love that sets all peo - ple free,
2 We sing a love that seeks an - oth - er's good,
3 We sing a love, un - flinch - ing, un - a - fraid
4 We sing a love that, wan - dering, will not rest
5 We sing the Ho - ly Spir - it, full of love,

that blows like wind, that burns like scorch - ing flame,
that longs to serve and not to count the cost,
to be it - self, de - spite an - oth - er's wrath,
un - til it finds its way, its home, its source,
who seeks out scars of an - cient bit - ter - ness,

Text: June Boyce-Tillman, 1993. © *1993 Stainer & Bell Ltd., admin. Hope Publishing Co.*
Music: Alfred Morton Smith, 1941. © *Estate of Doris Wright Smith.*

10 10 10 10
SURSUM CORDA

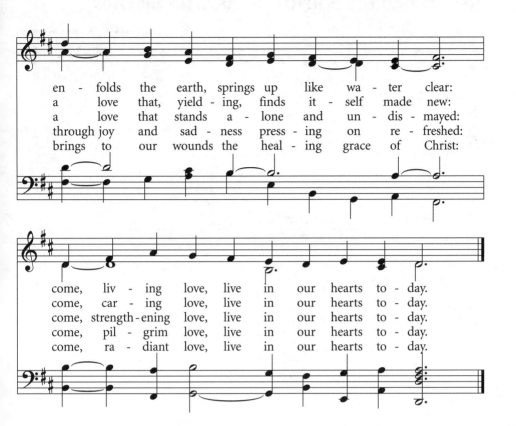

en - folds the earth, springs up like wa - ter clear:
a love that, yield - ing, finds it - self made new:
a love that stands a - lone and un - dis - mayed:
through joy and sad - ness press - ing on re - freshed:
brings to our wounds the heal - ing grace of Christ:

come, liv - ing love, live in our hearts to - day.
come, car - ing love, live in our hearts to - day.
come, strength - ening love, live in our hearts to - day.
come, pil - grim love, live in our hearts to - day.
come, ra - diant love, live in our hearts to - day.

164 When the Spirit/*Si el Espíritu de Dios*

When the Spir-it of the Lord moves in my soul I'll sing
Si el Es-pí-ri-tu de Dios se mue-ve en mi, yo can-

just as Da-vid sang. I'll sing, I'll sing, I'll
to co-mo Da-vid. Yo can-to, yo can-to, yo

sing just as Da-vid sang. I'll sing, I'll
can to co-mo Da-vid. Yo can-to, yo

sing, I'll sing just as Da-vid sang.
can - to, yo can-to co-mo Da-vid!

2	...praise(d)	2	*Yo alabo*
3	...pray(ed)	3	*Yo oro*
4	...jump(ed)	4	*Yo salto*
5	...dance(d)	5	*Yo danzo*
6	...laugh(ed)	6	*Yo rio*

Text: As taught by Guillermo of El Salvador to Becca Whitla in Toronto, 2007.
  English text by Becca Whitla, ©.
Music: Anon, Latin America, as taught by Guillermo of the San Esteban community in Toronto, 2007.

Irregular

Shout for Joy! 165

1 Shout for joy! The Lord has let us feast;
2 No more doubt - ing, no more sense - less dread:
3 Cel - e - brate with saints who dine on high,
4 Praise the Mak - er, praise the Mak - er's Son,

heaven's own fare has fed the last and least;
God's good self has graced our wine and bread;
wit - nes - ses that love can nev - er die.
praise the Spir - it— Three yet ev - er One;

Christ's own peace is shared a - gain on earth;
all the won - der heaven has kept in store
"Hal - le - lu - jah!"—thus their voic - es ring:
praise the God whose food and friends a - vow

is shared on earth;
has kept in store
their voic - es ring:
whose friends a - vow

God the Spir - it fills us with new worth.
now is ours to keep for ev - er - more.
noth - ing less in gra - ti - tude we bring.
heaven starts here! The king - dom beck - ons now!

Text: John L. Bell and Graham Maule, 1989.
Music: John L. Bell, 1989.
Text and music © 1989 WGRG c/o Iona Community, GIA Publications, Inc., agent.

99 99
LANSDOWNE

166 Hey ney yana

Hey ney ya - na, hey ney ya - na, hey ney ya - na,

Fine

hey ya hey yo, hey ya hey yo.

1 I walk in beau - ty, yes I do, yes I do. I
2 I leave in beau - ty, yes I do, yes I do. I

talk in beau - ty, yet I do, yes I do. I
sleep in beau - ty, yes I do, yes I do. I

D.C.

sing of beau - ty, hey ya hey yo, hey ya hey yo.
dream of beau - ty, hey ya hey yo, hey ya hey yo.

The syllables in the chorus of this song of respect for Creation are vocables, non-lexical syllables meant as vehicles for praise. Try this song unaccompanied or with a hand drum accenting the beginning of each measure.

Text and music: Brooke Medicine Eagle, ©; as taught by Leonard EagleCloud.

Irregular
HEY NEY YANA

Let Us Speak the Unsearchable Riches

Let us speak the un-search-a - ble rich - es of Christ, through our
sing - ing, our pray - ing, our sto - ries, with de -
light in your will, as we walk in your way, may we
love you, may we know you, may we show you.

Text: Jan and David Buley, 2002.
Music: David Buley, 2002. *Text and music* © 2002 Rublemusic Co.

12 10 12 12
FUNDY

168 May the God of Hope Go with Us

May the God of hope go with us ev - ery day,
¡Dios de la es - pe - ran - za, da - nos go - zo y paz!
Que le Dieu de l'es - pér - ance é - claire nos jours

fill - ing all our lives with love and joy and peace.
Al mun - do en cri - sis, ha - bla tu ver - dad.
rem - plis - sant nos vi - es de sa joie, sa paix.

May the God of jus - tice speed us on our way,
Dios de la jus - ti - cia, mán - da - nos tu luz,
Que le Dieu de la jus - tice et de l' - amour

bring - ing light and hope to ev - ery land and race.
luz y es - pe - ran - za en la os - cu - ri - dad.
nous mon - tre le chem - in de la vé - ri - té.

Text: English and Spanish text: Alvin Schutmaat, 1984;
French tr. Andrew Donaldson, 1996. *French tr.* © 1996 The Presbyterian Church in Canada.
Music: Argentine trad. melody.

11 11 11 11 with refrain
ARGENTINA

169 Sent Out in Jesus' Name/*Enviado soy de Dios*

Sent out in Je-sus' name, our hands are read-y now to
En - via - do soy de Dios, mi ma - no lis - ta es - tá pa - ra

make the world the place in which the king-dom comes. The
cons - tru - ir con El un mun - do fra - ter - nal. Los

an - gels can - not change a world of hurt and pain in -
án - ge - les no son en - via - dos a cam - biar un

Text: José Aguiar; Eng. trans. Jorge Maldonado, 1991.
© *1988 Abingdon Press, admin. Music Services.*
Music: Central American trad.; arr. *More Voices,* 2007. *Arr.* © *The United Church of Canada.*

12 12 12 12D
ENVIADO

to a world of love, of jus-tice and of peace. The
mun - do de do - lor por un mun - do de paz. _Me_

task is ours to do, to set it real - ly free. O,
ha to - ca - do a mi ha - cer - lo rea - li - dad; _a -_

help us to o - bey, and car - ry out your will.
yú - da - me, Se - ñor, a ha - cer tu vo - lun - tad.

170 *Sizohamba naye*/We Will Walk with God

1 Si - zo - ham - ba na - ye, wo wo wo, si - zo - ham - ba na - ye.
2 We will walk with God, my broth - ers, we will walk with God.
3 We will walk with God, my sis - ters, we will walk with God.

Ngom - hla wen - ja - bu - la si - zo - ham - ba na - ye.
We will go re - joic - ing till the king - dom has come.

Ngom - bla wen - ja - bu - la si - zo - ham - ba na - ye.
We will go re - joic - ing till the king - dom has come.

Text: Swaziland trad., trans. John L. Bell, 2002.
Trans. © 2002 WGRG c/o Iona Community, GIA Publications, Inc., agent.
Music: Swaziland traditional.

96 96 66 66
SIZOHAMBA NAYE

When You Go from Here

When you go from here, when you go from here, live with jus - tice, love with mer - cy, hum - bly walk in God's care.

Text and music: Linnea Good, 1991, alt. © 1991 Borealis Music.

Irregular
WHEN YOU WALK

172 May the Love of the Lord

May the love of the Lord rest up-on your soul.

May God's love dwell in you, through-out ev - ery day. May God's coun - te - nance shine up-on you

Text: Maria Ling, 1990, ©.
Music: Lim Swee Hong, 1990, ©. *Admin. General Board of Global Ministries t/a GBG Musik.*

Irregular
SOON T

and be gra - cious to you. May God's Spir - it

Am7   C/D   G2   G2   G2/B

be up - on you as you leave this place.

C6   G2/B   Am7   C/D   G2

Salamun/May Peace Be with You

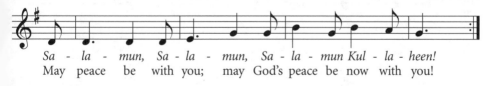

Sa - la - mun, Sa - la - mun, Sa - la - mun Kul - la - heen!
May peace be with you; may God's peace be now with you!

Arabic pronounciation: Sah-lah-moon koo-lah-heen.

Text: Author unknown; English para. S T Kimbrough, Jr., 2004. © 2004 GIA Publications, Inc.
Music: Melody Lebanese trad.

174 God Bless to Us Our Bread

Text: Spanish text: Federico Pagura; English tr. John L. Bell.

Irregular

Music: Argentine trad. melody; arr. John L. Bell. *Spanish text © Frederico Pagura and The Iona Community;*
English. tr. and music arr. © 1997 WGRG c/o Iona Community, GIA Publications, Inc., agent.

Almighty God, to You All Hearts Are Open 175

Music: Gord Johnson, 2004, ©.

176 Glory to God

Glo-ry to God in the high-est, and peace to his peo-ple on earth. Lord God, heaven-ly king, al-might-y God and Fa-ther, we wor-ship you, we give you thanks, we praise you for your glo-ry. Lord Je-sus Christ, on-ly Son of the Fa-ther, Lord God, Lamb of God, you take a-

Music: *New Life Mass*, Michael Capon, 2012, ©.

177 Glory to God/*Gloire à Dieu*

Leader

Glo-ry to God, glo-ry to God, glo-ry in the high-est!
Gloi-re à Dieu, gloi-re à Dieu, gloi-re et lou-an-ge!

All

Glo-ry to God, glo-ry to God, glo-ry in the high-est!
Gloi-re à Dieu, gloi-re à Dieu, gloi-re et lou-an-ge!

Leader   All

To God be glo-ry for-ev-er! To God be glo-ry for-ev-er!
À Dieu la gloire é-ter-nel-le. À Dieu la gloire é-ter-nel-le.

Leader   Leader

Al-le-lu-ia! A-men!   Al-le-lu-ia! A-men!

Group 1

Al-le-lu-ia! A-men! Al-le-lu-ia! A-men!

Leader

Al-le-lu-ia! A-men!

Groups 1 and 2   Groups 1, 2 & 3

Al-le-lu-ia! A-men! Al-le-lu-ia! A-men! Al-le-lu-ia! A-men!

Al-le-lu-ia! A-men! Al-le-lu-ia! A-men!

Music: Peruvian trad.

¡Gloria, Gloria, Gloria!/Glory, Glory, Glory 178

¡Glo - ria, glo - ria, glo - ria en las al tur - as a Dios!
Glo - ry, glo - ry, glo - ry, glo - ry be to God on high!

Y en la tie - rra paz pa - ra a-qué - llos que a - ma el Se - ñor.
And on earth peace to all peo - ple in whom God is well pleased.

Accompaniment patterns

Congas

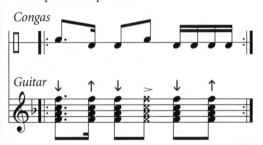

Guitar

Text: Luke 2:14.
Music: Pablo Sosa, 1988. © 1989 GIA Publications, Inc.

179 Kyrie eleison

Music: *St. Bridget Setting*, John L. Bell, 1998.
© 1998 WGRG c/o Iona Community, GIA Publications, Inc., agent.

Lord, Have Mercy 180

Lord, have mer - cy. Lord, have mer - cy.

Christ, have mer - cy. Christ, have mer - cy.

Lord, have mer - cy, Lord, have mer - cy.

This Kyrie may be sung with or without optional petitions.
If petitions are used, they may be said or sung.

Music: Ian Forrester, ©.

Lord, Have Mercy 181

Lord, have mer - cy. Lord, have mer -

cy. Lord, have mer - cy.

Music: Mark MacDonald; adapt. Frances Densmore. © *Church Publishing.*

182 Lord, Have Mercy/*Wey a hey a heyaheyo*

Music: David Buley, 2010. © *2010 Rublemusic Co.*

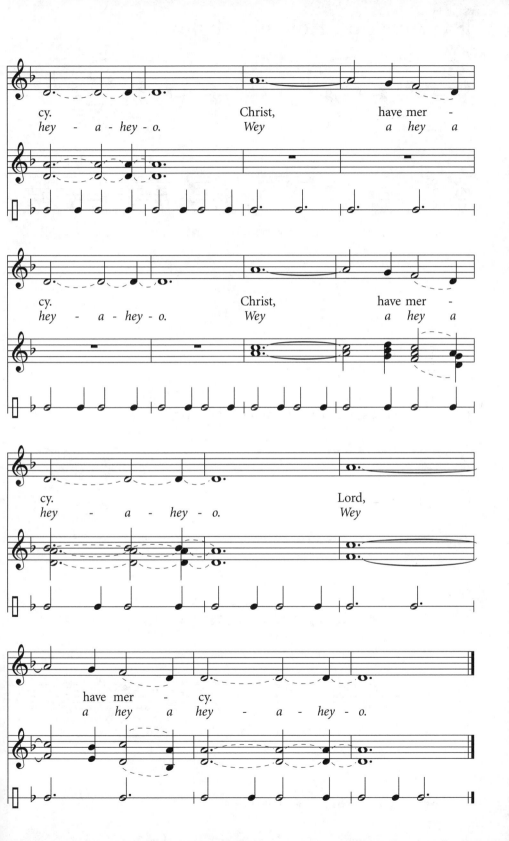

ACT OF PRAISE Trisagion

183 Holy God, Holy and Mighty

Music: trad. Russian Orthodox.

ACT OF PRAISE Trisagion

184 Holy God, Holy and Mighty

To be sung three times.

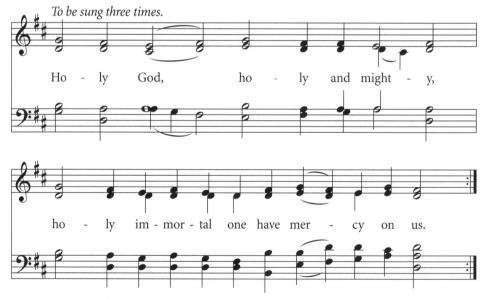

Music: Serbian trad., arr. Walter G. Obleschuk, 1998, alt., ©.

O Holy God, Holy and Immortal 185

1,3 O ho - ly God, ho - ly and im - mor - tal,
2 O ho - ly God, ho - ly and al - might - y,

1,3 O ho - ly God, ho - ly and im - mor - tal,
2 O ho - ly God, ho - ly and al - might - y,

God, have mer - cy on us.
God, have mer - cy on us.

God, have mer - cy on us.
God, have mer - cy on us.

Text: Trad. liturgical text.
Music: As taught by Islam Pilpani, Lenjer village, Georgia;
transc. Becca Whitla and Alan Gasser, 1998. *Music © 1998 Creative Commons.*

GEORGIA

186 Alleluia, Lord, I Love the Place

Al - le - lu - ia, al - le - lu - ia, al - le - lu - ia, al - le - lu - ia, al - le -
lu - ia, al - le - lu - ia, al - le - lu - ia, al-le - lu - ia, al - le - lu - ia.
Lord, I love the place in which you dwell, al - le - lu - ia, al - le -
lu - ia. And the place where your glo - ry lives. For your love is be-
fore my eyes; I have walked faith - ful - ly with you.

Text: from Psalm 26.
Music: *Red Lake Mass*, Monte Mason; adapt. Frances Densmore. © *Church Publishing.*

Amen, Amen, It Shall Be So   187

1 Blest are the poor in spir - it, the
2 Blest are the sor - row - ful, the sor - row - ful, they
3 Blest are the gen - tle, the gen - tle, the
4 Blest are the hun - gry for jus - tice, they
5 Blest are the mer - ci - ful, the mer - ci - ful, they

Words sung as antiphon, notes hummed as verse accompaniment.

Am   Dm⁷   G   CM⁷

A - men, a - men, it shall be so! A -

king - dom of heaven is theirs.
shall be com - for - ted.
earth shall be their own.
shall be sat - is - fied.
shall find mer - cy shown.

F   Bm⁷(♭5)   E

men, al - le - lu - ia!

6   Blest are the pure in heart,
    for they shall see their God.

7   Blest are the earth's peacemakers,
    each one shall be God's child.

8   Blest are those victimized for doing good,
    the kingdom of heaven is theirs.

Text and music: John L. Bell, after Matthew 5:3–10.

188 Listen Now for the Gospel!

Text: Zimbabwean liturgical acclamation; transc. John L. Bell, 2002.
Transcr. © 2002 WGRG c/o Iona Community, GIA Publications, Inc., agent.
Music: Zimbabwean trad.

Al - le - lu - ia, al - le - lu - ia. Al - le - lu - ia, al - le -

lu - ia. Al - le - lu - ia, al - le - lu - ia, al - le - lu - ia.

Verse

Music: Melody Honduras trad.; arr. John L. Bell, 1995.
Arr. © 1995 WGRG c/o Iona Community, GIA Publications, Inc., agent.

190   Alleluia

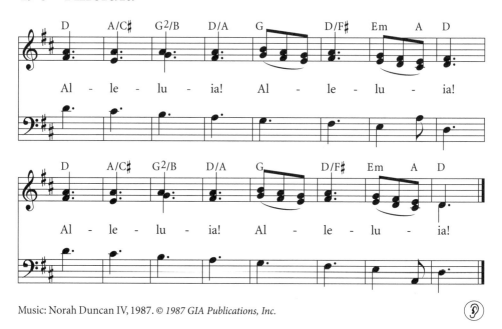

Al - le - lu - ia! Al - le - lu - ia!

Al - le - lu - ia! Al - le - lu - ia!

Music: Norah Duncan IV, 1987. © 1987 GIA Publications, Inc.

191   Heleluyan

He - le - lu - yan, he - le - lu - yan.

He - le, he - le - lu - yan.

He - le - lu - yan, he - le - lu - yan,

he - le, he - le - lu - yan.

Text and music: As sung by the Muscogee Creek Nation. Transcr. Kenneth Hull, 2020, ©.

Halle, Halle, Hallelujah! 192

Music: Melody Caribbean trad.; arr. John L. Bell, 1990.
Arr. © 1990 WGRG c/o Iona Community, GIA Publications, Inc., agent.

HALLE, HALLE

193 Alleluia

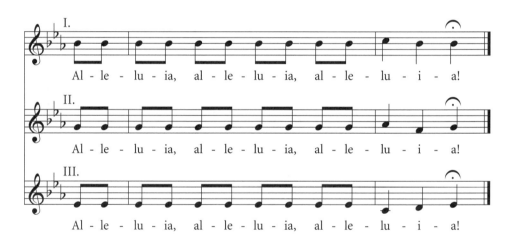

Music: Byzantine chant, arr. Jeffrey Honoré, 2006.

Alleluia/*Amen* 194

Al - le - lu - ia, al - le - lu - ia,
A - *men,* *a* - *men,* *a* - *men,* *a* - *men,*

al - le - lu - ia, al le - lu - ia.
a - *men,* *a* - *men,* *a* - *men.*

Music: Moosonee Service, David Buley, 2010. © 2010 Rublemusic Co.

195 Open Your Ears, O Faithful People

1 O - pen your ears, O faith-ful peo - ple, o - pen your ears and
2 They who have ears to hear the mes-sage, they who have ears, now

hear God's Word. O - pen your hearts, O roy - al priest - hood,
let them hear. They who would learn the way of wis - dom,

God has come to you. God has spo - ken
let them hear God's Word. To - rah o - ra,

to the peo - ple, hal - le - lu - jah! God has spo - ken
To - rah o - ra, hal - le - lu - jah! To - rah o - ra,

Text: Hasidic trad.; trans. Willard F. Jabusch, 1966.
© 1966, 1982 Willard F. Jabusch, admin. OCP Publications.
Music: Hasidic trad.; arr. Evangelical Lutheran Worship, 2006. © 2006 Augsburg Fortress.

95 95 with Refrain
YISRAEL V'ORAITA

words of wis-dom, hal - e - lu - jah! jah!
To - rah o - ra, hal - le - lu - jah! jah!

Alleluia 196

Al - le - lu - ia, al - le - lu - ia, al - le -

lu - ia, al - le - lu - ia. Al - le - lu - ia, al - le -

lu - ia, al - le - lu - ia, al - le - lu - ia.

Music: Jerry Sinclair, 1972. © 1972, renewed 2000 Manna Music, Inc.

197 Alleluia

Choir, repeat All

Al - le - lu - ia, al - le - lu - ia! Al - le - lu - ia, al - le - lu - ia! Al - le - lu - ia, al -

Music: Peter Jones, 1994, ©, *admin. OCP Publications.*

le - le - lu - ia! Al - le - lu - ia, al - le - lu - ia!

Verse

All After the verse

Al - le - lu - ia, al - le - lu - ia! Al - le - lu - ia, al -

Choir

Al - le - lu - ia, al - le - lu - ia! Al - le - lu - ia, al -

Kyrie Eleison on Our World 198

Text and music: Larry Olson. © 1989 Dakota Road Music.

Leader/Choir

1 For peace in the world, for the
2 That we may live out your im -
3 For peace in our hearts, for
4 For your Spir - it to guide: that you

C#m

health of the church, for the
pas - sioned re - sponse to the
peace in our homes, for
cen - ter our lives in the

B

u - ni - ty of all; for
hun - gry and the poor; that
friends and fam - i - ly; for
wa - ter and the Word; that you

A   E

this ho - ly house, for all who wor - ship and praise,
we may live out truth and jus - tice and grace,
life and for love, for our work and our play,
nour - ish our souls with your bod - y and blood,

let us pray to the Lord,

let us pray to the Lord.

to Refrain

199 God Ever-faithful, God Ever-merciful

Refrain: All

God ev-er-faith - ful, God ev-er-mer-ci - ful,

God of your peo - ple, hear our prayer.

Cantor

1 For those who lead and guide the Church of Christ;
2 For faith - ful wit - ness, fel - low - ship in love;
3 For those who guide the na - tions of the earth;
4 For those who seek and serve the com - mon good;

A selection of verses may be used.

Text and music: Michael Joncas, 1990. © 1990 GIA Publications, Inc.

to refrain

for	lov - ing	care,		we	pray	to	you,	O	Lord:
for	liv - ing	hope,		we	pray	to	you,	O	Lord:
that	wis - dom	reign,		we	pray	to	you,	O	Lord:
that	jus - tice	reign,		we	pray	to	you,	O	Lord:

Am   G/B   A⁷/C♯   D

5   For neighbours' needs, for shelter from the storm;
      for homes of peace, we pray to you, O Lord:

6   For those in sorrow, anguish, and despair;
      that they find hope, we pray to you, O Lord:

7   For those oppressed, for those who live in fear;
      that they be freed, we pray to you, O Lord:

8   For all the sick, the dying, and the dead,
      be life and grace, we pray to you, O Lord:

9   That we might live in peace from day to day;
      that wars will cease, we pray to you, O Lord:

10   That we stay faithful, open to your Word;
      your Kingdom come! We pray to you, O Lord:

11   For all the dreams held deep within our hearts;
      for all our needs, we pray to you, O Lord:

12   Enrusting all we are into your hands,
      we call your name, and pray to you, O Lord:

200 Ay, Ay Salidummay

Ay, ay sa - li - dum - may, let us give thanks to God.

The word "Salidummay" is an expression of joy.

Text and music: Philipines trad., transcr. and adapt. I-to Loh, ©.

201 Lord, in Your Mercy

Lord, in your mer - cy hear our prayer.

Music: John L. Bell, 1995. © 1995, 1998 WGRG c/o Iona Community, GIA Publications, Inc., agent.

202 Lord, in Your Mercy

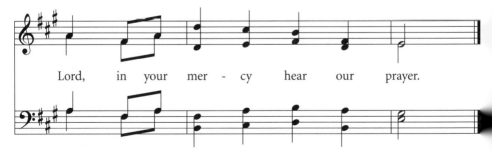

Lord, in your mer - cy hear our prayer.

Music: John Harper. © 2000 The Royal School of Church Music.

Hear Our Prayer 203

Hear our prayer, hear our prayer,
Lord, make us whole: peace to all
peo - ple, hope for each soul. God of grace,
in this place, hear now our prayer.

Text and music: Paul Andress, 2006. © 2006 Augsburg Fortress.

204 Remember Your Mercy, Lord

Re - mem - ber, re - mem - ber your mer - cy, Lord. Re -
mem - ber, re - mem - ber your mer - cy, Lord.
Hear your peo - ple's prayer as they call to you: re -

Text and music: Paul Inwood, 1981, ©. *Published by OCP Publications.*

mem - ber, re - mem - ber your mer - cy Lord.

Gbemi, Jesu/*Lift Me, Jesus* 205

Gbe - mi, gbe - mi, Je - su. A - men.

Lift me, lift me, Je - sus. A - men.

Optional stanzas

Bless me…
Heal me…
Help me…
Save me…

Text and music: Yoruba, author and composer unknown.

GBEMI, JESU

206 Mayenziwe/*Your Will Be Done*

Ma - ye - nzi - we 'nta - ndo ya - kho. Ma -
Your will be done on earth, O Lord. Your
Ma - ye
Your will

ye - nzi - we 'nta - ndo ya - kho. Ma - ye - nzi -
will be done on earth, O Lord. Your will be
Ma - ye
Your will

we 'nta - ndo ya - kho. Ma - ye - nzi - we 'nta -
done on earth, O Lord. Your will be done on

ndo ya - kho. Ma - ye - nzi - we 'nta - ndo ya - kho.
earth, O Lord. Your will be done on earth, O Lord.

Text: South African, based on the Lord's Prayer.
Music: South African trad., as taught by Gobingca George Mxadana; arr. John L. Bell.
Arr. © 1990 WGRG c/o Iona Community, GIA Publications, Inc., agent.

88 88 8
MAYENZIWE

Kyrie eleison 207

Ky - ri - e   e - le - i - son,   Ky - ri - e   e - le - i - son,   Ky - ri -

e   e - le - i - son,   Ky - ri - ie   e - le - i - son.

Music: Melody Guarani trad., Paraguay; arr. Michael Capon, 2019, ©.

208 Kyrie eleison

Ky - ri - e, e - lei - son. Ky - ri - e e - lei - son.

Ky - ri - e e - lei - son. Ky - ri - e e - lei - son.

Music: Melody Dinah Reindorf, 1987, ©, *admin. Augsburg Fortress*; arr. Kenneth Hull, 2019, ©.

Music: John L. Bell, 1995. © 1995 WGRG c/o Iona Community, GIA Publications, Inc., agent.

210 Kindle a Flame to Lighten the Dark

Kin - dle a flame to light - en the dark and

take all fear a - way.

Text: John L. Bell and Graham Maule, 1987.
Music: John L. Bell, 1987.
Text and music © 1987 WGRG c/o Iona Community, GIA Publications, Inc., agent.

Hold Us in Your Grace 211

May be sung as two-part round.

*Alternative words: Peace, Love, etc.

Text: Keri K. Wehlander, 2007, ©.
Music: Keri K. Wehlander and Bruce Harding, 2007, ©.

212 Holy, Holy, Holy

Music: *St. Aidan Setting*, John L. Bell, 1998.
© 1998 WGRG c/o Iona Community, GIA Publications, Inc., agent.

213 Holy, Holy, Holy Lord

Music: *Mass of the City of Light*, Brigid Coult, 1990, ©.

214 *Santo es el Señor*/Holy Is the Lord

1   ¡San-to,   san-to,   san-to,
2 (¡Ho) - san-na,   ho - san-na,   ho - san-na,   ho -
1   Ho-ly,   ho-ly,   ho-ly,
2 (Ho) - san-na,   ho - san-na,   ho - san-na,   ho -

san-to,   san-to es el Se - ñor!   ¡San-to,   san-to,
san-na,   ho - san-na al Se - ñor!   ¡Ho-san-na,   ho-san-na,   ho-
ho - ly,   ho - ly   is   the   Lord!   Ho-ly,   ho-ly,
san-na,   ho - san-na   to   the   Lord!   Ho-san-na,   ho-san-na,   ho-

san - to,   san - to,   san - to es el Se - ñor!   Los
san - na,   ho - san - na,   ho - san - na al Se - ñor!   Ben -
ho - ly,   ho - ly,   ho - ly   is   the   Lord!   The
san - na,   ho - san - na,   ho - san - na   to   the   Lord!   Oh

Text: Traditional.
Music: Guatemala trad.; arr. Greg Scheer, 2008, ©.

án - ge - les y san - tos can-tan "San - to al Se - ñor." Y en-
di - to el que vie - ne en el nom-bre del Se - ñor. Y
an - gels fill the heav-ens with a song un - to the Lord. Cre-
bless - ed is the one who bring a mes-sage from the Lord. The

Am   Em   B⁷   E⁷

tie - ra nos u - ni - mos de al - a - ban - za y gra - ti -
can - ta co - mo an - ge les "San - to, san - to es el Se -
a - tion lifts its voice up in a song of gra - ti -
an - gels, hear them sing - ing: "Ho - ly, ho - ly is the

Am   Em   B⁷

tud.   2 Ho
ñor."
tude.   2 Ho
Lord."

Em

215 *Santo, santo, santo*/Holy, Holy, Holy

Le lo le lo lay lo. Le lo le lo lay lo. Le lo le lo lay lo lo le lo le lo lay.

Cantor first time, then all repeat.

San-to, san-to, san-to Dios de glo-ria y po-der.
Ho-ly, ho-ly, ho-ly, God of pow-er and might.

Cie - los y tie - rra pro-cla-man tu glo - ria.
Heav - en and earth are full of your glo - ry.

glo - ria. Ho-sa-na, ho-sa-na, ho-sa-na en los cie-los. Ho-
glo - ry. Ho-san-na, ho-san-na, ho-san-na in the high-est. Ho-

* The first 8 bars are optional, but can be inserted between any sections.

Music: Order de Predicadores.

216 Holy, Holy, Holy Lord

217 Holy, Holy, Holy Lord

Cantor

Ho - ly, ho - ly, ho - ly Lord,

All

Ho - ly, ho - ly, ho - ly Lord,

Gi - chi Ma - ni - doo,
God of power and might,

heav - en and earth are full of your glo - ry.

Ho - san - na in the high - est.

Bless-ed is the one who comes in the name of the Lord.

Ho - san - na in the high - - - est.

Music: *Red Lake Mass,* Monte Mason. © *Church Publishing.*

Holy, Holy, Holy Lord 218

1 Ho - ly, ho - ly, ho - ly Lord, God of power and might,
2 Bless - ed is the one who comes in the name of the Lord.

heaven and earth are full of your glo - ry. Ho - san - na in the high - est.
Ho - san - na in the high - est, ho - san - na in the high - est.

Text: English Language Liturgical Consultation, 1988, alt. © *1988 ELLC.*
Music: Kenneth George Finlay, adapt. Gordon Appleton. © *Broomhill Hyndland Parish Church.* GLENFINLAS

219 Holy, Holy, Holy Lord

Choir

Ho - ly, ho - ly, ho - ly Lord, God of pow'r and might,

All

Ho - ly, ho - ly, ho - ly Lord, God of pow'r and might,

heav'n and earth are full of your glo - ry. Ho -

san - na in the high - est, Ho - san - na in the high - est, Ho -

Choir

san - na in the high - est. Bless-ed is the one who comes in the

All

name of the Lord. Ho - san - na in the high - est, Ho -

san - na in the high - est, Ho - san - na in the high - est.

Music: French trad., 16th cent.; adapt. David Buley. © 2010 Rublemusic Co.

We Remember His Death   220

Music: *Moosonee Mass*, David Buley, 2010. © *2010 Rublemusic Co.*

221 Amen

A - men. A - men.

A - men, a - men, a - men.

Music: South African trad.

222 Ameni

A - men - i, a - men - i, a -

Ba-ba-ba-ba-bam, ba-ba-ba-ba-bam, ba-ba-ba-ba-

men, a - men, a - men, a - men - i.

bam, ba-bam, ba-bam, ba-ba-ba-ba-bam.

Music: Young men at Christ the New Man Parish, Ga-Rankuwa, South Africa, 1989; transcr. and arr. David Dargie, ©.

Lord's Prayer 223

Nossinan*/Our Father in heaven, hal-low'd be your Name, your kingdom come,

your will be done, on earth as in heav-en. Give us today our dai-ly bread.

Forgive us our sins as we forgive those who sin a-gainst us.

Save us from the time of tri-al, and deliver us from e-vil.

For the kingdom, the power, and the glory are yours, now and for ever.

A - men.

* Ojibway word. Option for "Our Father" pronounced noh-sih-nahn.

Music: Red Lake Mass, Monte Mason. © Church Publishing.

THE LORD'S PRAYER

224 Our Father in Heaven/*Abana alathifi ssama*

Text: Arabic text: Laila Constantine. Tr. and adapt. Anne Emile Zaki, Emily Brink, and Greg Scheer.
Music: Laila Constantine, arr. Greg Scheer.

Arabic text and music: © 2002 Songs of the Evangelical Presbyterian Church of Egypt, Synod of the Nile,
Council of Pastoral Work and Evangelism, admin. Faith Alive Christian Resources;
Tr., adapt. and arr. © 2008 Faith Alive Christian Resources.

Yours   is   the   king - dom,   yours   the   pow - er,
yours   is   the   glo - ry   now   and   ev - er.
Li - an - na   la - k̲al   mu - l - ka
Wal   quw - wa - ta   wal   ma - j - da

Our Fa - ther   in heav - en.   A - men.
Min al - a - zal   i - la al - a   bad.   A - min.

Alleluia, Christ Our Passover 225

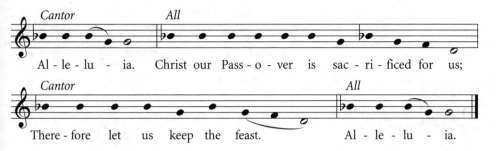

Music: *Red Lake Mass*, Monte Mason. © *Church Publishing.*

Lamb of God 226

Music: DIVINUM MYSTERIUM; adapt. David Buley, 2010. © *2010 Rublemusic Co.*

227 I Am the Bread of Life

Text and music: Tom Kaczmarek; arr. Paul A. Tate, 2005.

Here Is the Bread 228

1 Here is the bread that is bro - ken for you.
2 Here is the cup that I of - fer to you.
3 This is the task I am giv - ing to you:
4 Eat this and drink in re - mem - brance of me.

Take it and eat, take it and eat.
Take it and drink, take it and drink.
be full of love, be full of love.
I am the way; I am the way.

Here is the bread that is bro - ken for you; if you
Here is the cup that I of - fer to you; come re -
This is the task I am giv - ing to you: love each
Eat this and drink in re - mem - brance of me till we

eat you will hun - ger no more.
ceive the for - give - ness of sins.
oth - er as I have loved you.
eat in the king - dom of God.

Text and music: Celah K. Pence, 2002, ©.

10 4 4 10 9
HERE IS THE BREAD

229 Here Is Bread

1 Here is bread, here is wine, Christ is with us,
2 Here is grace, here is peace, Christ is with us,
3 Here we are, joined in one, Christ is with us,

he is with us. Break the bread, taste the wine,
he is with us. Know his grace, find his peace,
he is with us. We'll pro - claim till he comes

Refrain

Christ is with us here.
feast on Je - sus here.
Je - sus cru - ci - fied.

In this bread,

Text and music: Graham Kendrick, 1991. © 1991 Make Way Music.

68 65 with refrain
HERE IS BREAD

230 Lamb of God

Music: *Moosonee Service*, David Buley, 2010. © *2010 Moosonee Service.*

God, you take a - way the sins of the world:

God, you take a - way the sins of the world:

God, you take a - way the sins of the world:

God, you take a - way the sins of the world:

grant us peace, grant us peace.

grant us peace, grant us peace.

grant us peace, grant us peace.

grant us peace, grant us peace.

231 Lamb of God

Lamb of God, you take away the sins of the world: (on us.) Lamb of God, you take away the sins of the have mer-cy on us. grant us peace, world: have mer-cy world: grant us grant us peace, grant us peace. peace, grant us peace, grant us peace.

Music: *St. Bride Setting*, The Iona Community.
© 1995 WGRG c/o Iona Community, GIA Publications, Inc., agent.

Copyright Holders

The following companies and institutions hold copyrights for material included in this collection. Contact information for individual copyright holders may be obtained through the Rights and Permission Department of Church Publishing, Incorporated.

Augsburg Fortress
(including Lutheran Book of Worship, Ton Vis Produktion AB)
www.augsburgfortress.org

Choristers Guild
www.choristersguild.org

Church Publishing
(including The Church Pension Fund)
www.churchpublishing.org

EMI CMG Publishing
(including Thankyou Music)
www.capitolcmgpublishing.com

Evangelical Lutheran Church in Canada
www.elcic.ca

Faber Music Ltd.
www.fabermusic.com

Faith Alive Christian Resources
www.faithaliveresources.org

General Board of Global Ministries
umcmission.org

GIA Publications, Inc.
(including Christian Conference of Asia, Iona Community, Les Presses de Taizé, Walton Music Corp., and World Library Publications)
www.giamusic.com

Hinshaw Music, Inc.
www.hinshawmusic.com

Hope Publishing Co.
(including Stainer & Bell Ltd., The Hymn Society, and The Jubilate Group)
www.hopepublishing.com

Integrity's Hosanna! Music
(including Daybreak Music)
www.integritymusic.com

International Commission on English in the Liturgy
www.icelweb.org

Kevin Mayhew, Ltd.
www.kevinmayhew.com

Make Way Music
www.grahamkendrick.co.uk

Manna Music, Inc.
mannamusicinc.com

Maranatha Praise, Inc.
www.maranathamusic.com

MennoMedia Inc.
www.mennomedia.org

Music Services
(including Abingdon Press, and Mercy/Vineyard Publishing)
musicservices.org

OCP Publications
www.ocp.org

Oxford University Press
global.oup.com

Royal School of Church Music
www.rscm.org.uk

Selah Publishing Co., Inc.
www.selahpub.com

The Pilgrim Press
www.thepilgrimpress.com

The Presbyterian Church in Canada
presbyterian.ca

United Church of Canada
united-church.ca

Wayne Leupold Editions, Inc.
theleupoldfoundation.org

Westminster John Knox Press
www.wjkbooks.com

World Council of Churches
www.oikoumene.org

Subject Index

Tune Names